W9-AYD-689

From Abenaki to Zuni

A Dictionary of Native American Tribes

OTHER BOOKS BY EVELYN WOLFSON:

American Indian Tools and Ornaments (David McKay Co., Inc.)
American Indian Utensils (David McKay Co., Inc.)
American Indian Habitats, co-author Nancy Simon (David McKay Co., Inc.)
Growing Up Indian (Walker and Company)
Environmental Education: A Manual for Elementary Educators, co–author Barbara Robinson (Teachers College Press)

FROM ABENAKI TO ZUNI

A DICTIONARY OF NATIVE AMERICAN TRIBES

By Evelyn Wolfson

Illustrated by William Sauts Bock

973.004
Wol

18218

WALKER AND COMPANY
NEW YORK, NEW YORK

Copyright © 1988 by Evelyn Wolfson

All rights reserved. No part of this book may be reproduced or transmitted in any form or by any means, electronic or mechanical, including photocopying, recording, or by any information storage and retrieval system, without permission in writing from the Publisher.

First published in the United States of America in 1988 by the Walker Publishing Company, Inc.

Published simultaneously in Canada by Thomas Allen and Son, Canada, Limited, Markham, Ontario.

Library of Congress Cataloging-in-Publication Data

Wolfson, Evelyn.
From Abenaki to Zuni: a dictionary of native American tribes / by Evelyn Wolfson: illustrated by William Sauts Bock.
p. cm.
Bibliography: p.
Includes index.
Summary: An alphabetical identification of sixty-eight of the larger North American Indian tribes, describing their habitats, social life and customs, food, means of travel, and modern descendants. Includes drawings and maps.
ISBN 0-8027-6789-3. ISBN 0-8027-6790-7 (lib. bdg.)
1. Indians of North America—Dictionaries, Juvenile. [1. Indians of North America—Dictionaries.] I. Bock, William Sauts, 1939– ill. II. Title.
E76.2.W65 1988 973'.0497'0032—dc19 87-27875

Printed in the United States of America

10 9 8 7 6 5 4 3 2

Text design by Laurie McBarnette

Contents

Acknowledgments

My sincere thanks to all the people who helped with this dictionary:

Professor Vine Deloria, Jr., The University of Arizona, Tucson; Professor W. W. Newcomb, Jr., University of Texas at Austin; Dr. Sven Liljeblad, Reno, Nevada; Dr. Brigham Madsen, Salt Lake City, Utah; Dr. Floyd O'Neill, University of Utah; Professor Charles Hudson, The University of Georgia, Athens; Professor Mary Murphy, Framingham State College, Massachusetts; Rosemary Carlton, Interpretive Specialist, Sheldon Jackson Museum, Sitka, Alaska; and Dr. Bennett Simon, Newton, Massachusetts.

I am especially grateful to Sandy Hoyt, Children's Librarian, Burlington Public Library and Dr. Jeffrey P. Brain, Curator, Peabody Museum of Archaeology and Ethnology, Harvard University, for reading and critiquing the entire manuscript.

Foreword

Evelyn Wolfson has written extensively and successfully about North American Indians for the younger audience. *From Abenaki to Zuni: A Dictionary of Native American Tribes* skillfully guides the reader through the diversity of Indian peoples and their cultures. I heartily recommend this handy reference for those just beginning to explore the world of the Indian.

Jeffrey P. Brain, Ph.D.
Peabody Museum of Archaeology and Ethnology
Harvard University
Cambridge, Massachusetts

MAJOR CULTURAL AREAS

DA
MONTAGNAIS-NASKAPI
MICMAC
MALISEET
PENNACOOK
ALGONQUIAN
OJIBWA (CHIPPEWA)
ABENAKI
HURON
LAKE SUPERIOR
MENOMINEE
L. HURON
MASSACHUSETT
WAMPANOAG
NARRAGANSETT
MOHAWK
OTTAWA
L. ONTARIO
ONEIDA
ONONDAGA
PEQUOT
WINNEBAGO
SAUK
FOX
KICKAPOO
POTAWATOMIE
L. MICHIGAN
L. ERIE
CAYUGA
SENECA
DELAWARE
MISSISSIPPI
NORTHEAST
SUSQUEHANNA
ILLINI
OHIO R.
ATLANTIC OCEAN
IOWA
OTO
SHAWNEE
CHEROKEE
INS
KIOWA
CHICKASAW
CATAWBA
OSAGE
CREEK
CADDO
SOUTHEAST
WICHITA
CHOCTAW
CHITAMACHA
SEMINOLE
GULF of MEXICO
N
Sauts

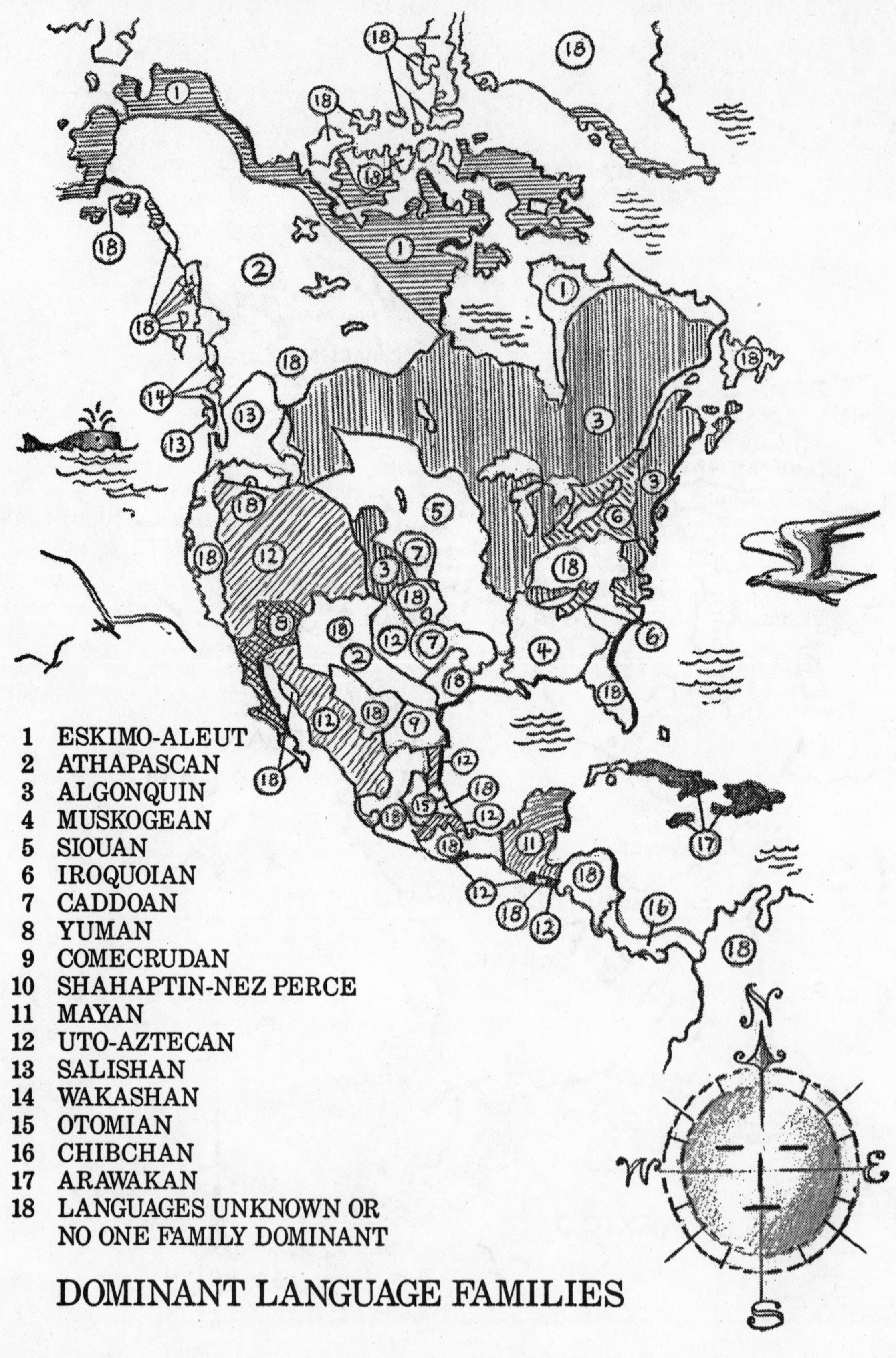

DOMINANT LANGUAGE FAMILIES

Introduction

The 68 North American Indian tribes, or bands, listed alphabetically in this dictionary, represent only a fraction of the Native Americans who were living in the United States, Canada, and Mexico when European explorers and settlers first came to the New World. Tribes not listed in the Table of Contents may be found in the Index, where readers are directed to tribes that share a similar lifestyle.

This dictionary is intended to be a reference tool for young readers, a simple, easy-to-follow source of information on a number of Native American tribes. In each entry, tribal names are spelled phonetically and the meaning of the name is included if it is known. Europeans often spelled Indian names the way they sounded and many have no meaning. The Indian meaning, however, is included whenever possible. There are also brief descriptions of the environment, villages, house types, food sources, methods of transportation, types of clothing, mythological heros, major ceremonies, and religious beliefs of each tribe at the time of European contact. Religious beliefs and ceremonies are described in the present tense because many Native Americans continue to observe their traditional religions.

Although the entries are as accurate as research permits, it should be noted that historical documentation about tribal differences is imprecise. Most headings at the top of each entry are expanded in the text, with the exception of travel, which lists only the mode of transportation and when known, the materials used to build the craft. Food is listed in each heading in the approximate order of its importance, but sometimes the order is questionable.

To complete each entry, the author has included a brief historical review of what later happened to the tribe—information regarding reservations, treaty settlements, and payment for tribal land claims. Many Native Americans do not live on reservations today or in areas traditionally occupied by their people, but live instead in typical neighborhoods the same as other Americans.

This dictionary does not pretend to include all aspects of Native American history. It is intended to inspire children to look further and fill in the gaps.

From Abenaki to Zuni:

A Dictionary of Native American Tribes

ABENAKI

(ahbeh-NAHKEE)

MEANING OF NAME: Dawn land people or easterners

CULTURE AREA: Northeast

LOCATION: Canada, Vermont, Maine, and southern Massachusetts

DWELLING TYPES: Longhouses and wigwams

CLOTHING MATERIAL: Skins

TRANSPORTATION: Snowshoes and birch-bark canoes

FOOD: Meat, fish, wild plants, and corn

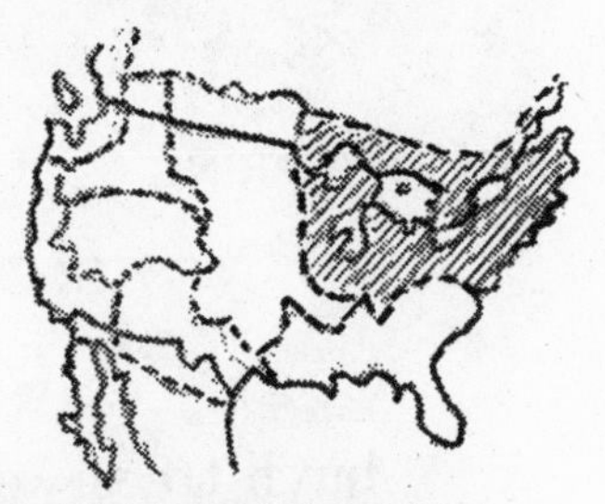

The Abenaki lived along rivers and streams that stretched toward the rocky coast of the Atlantic Ocean. Lush deciduous forests, cattail marshes, and fields of grass bordered the fast-moving waters. The trees in the forest were home to many animals and provided an unending source of wild foods and building materials. The Abenaki built small villages high above the water on bluffs, which offered them protection against attack. In western portions of their territory, birch trees grew abundantly, and the bark was used to cover great longhouses, housing several related families, which they framed with saplings. The hardwood forests of the region contained trees that could not be cut with stone axes, so young flexible trees served for wigwam frames. Beyond the dense woodlands of the west and north, food sources and

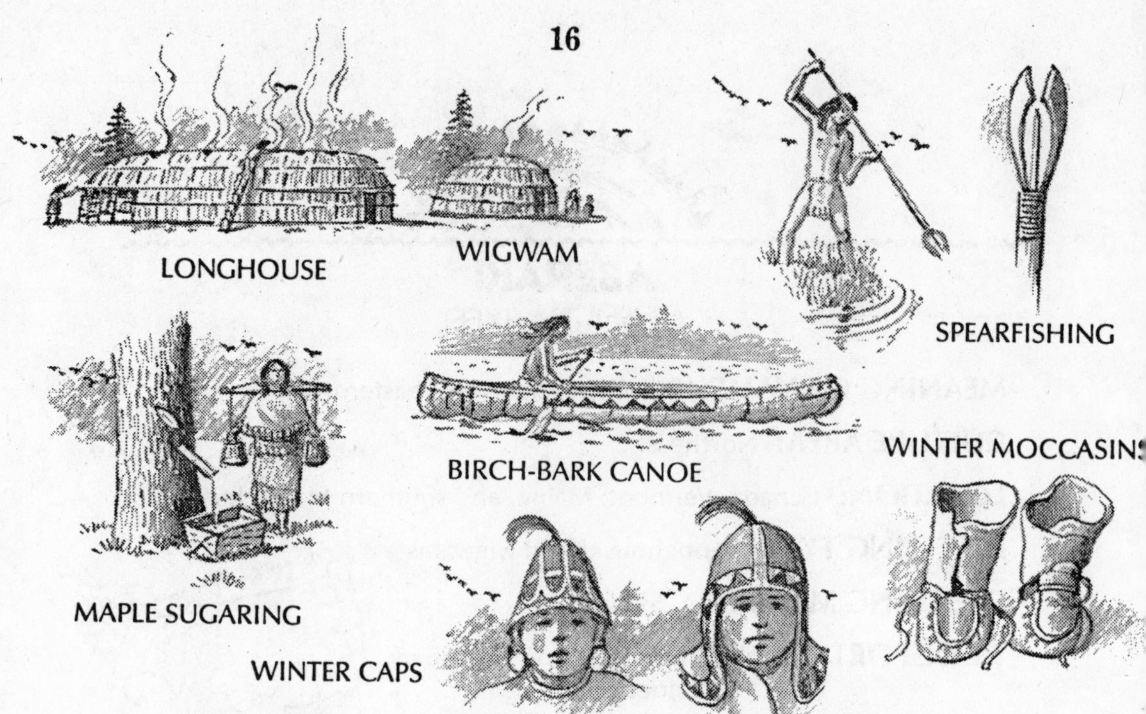

birch trees were limited, so the Eastern bands built single-family, dome-shaped, bark-covered wigwams, which they called witus.

The Abenaki hunted, fished, and gathered wild foods the year round. Moose, deer, bear, caribou, and smaller animals were easy to hunt. In February, western bands camped in the maple sugar groves while they collected sap, which they boiled down to syrup and candy. In spring, the men fished for salmon, eel, and alewifes; and in summer they traveled to the coast, where they dug for shellfish and hunted seals, porpoises, and birds. From canoes in shallow water, young boys speared lobsters and crabs. In fall, women gathered berries, nuts, and wild greens, which were plentiful throughout the area. Fertile inland flatlands encouraged some bands to plant small gardens of corn and tobacco.

In summer the men wore tanned buckskin breechcloths and the women wore knee-length leather skirts.

In colder weather, they added fur robes or sleeveless coats that resembled vests, and they wore moosehide moccasins, leggings, and caps. They insulated their moccasins by lining them with rabbit fur.

The Abenaki believe in Gluscap, and Trickster, the Raccoon, legendary characters who are depicted as both good and bad beings. The old men of the tribe told stories during the long winter months when man's natural enemies, the water monsters, are trapped under the ice and cannot hear.

Tribes of the Abenaki allied themselves with the French in an effort to control the region's fur trade. Throughout the 1600s and 1700s they successfully fought off Iroquois invaders, but they became victims of European diseases, which killed many of their people. When the English came to settle, the survivors fled to Canada.

Descendants of the Abenaki live in Old Town, Maine, and in Quebec, Canada.

ACOMA

(A-kehmuh)

MEANING OF NAME: People of the white rock

CULTURE AREA: Southwest

LOCATION: West central New Mexico

DWELLING TYPE: Multifamily adobe houses

CLOTHING MATERIALS: Skins and cotton cloth

TRANSPORTATION: Horses

FOOD: Corn, wild plants, and meat

The Acoma have lived on top of a 350-foot-high mesa in the same village of Acoma Pueblo for over eight hundred years. Their steep-sided mesa, carved from a large plateau thousands of years ago by a swift-moving river, stands like a defiant giant on the floor of an arid, treeless valley. To strangers, it is a hostile land, but it is home to dozens of spike-leaved plants, fat burrowing animals, and the Acoma, who know how to live on a minimum of water. Long ago the Acoma settled on the mesa top to protect themselves from raiders who came to steal their corn. Their three-story adobe homes, which are connected to one another like apartment houses, are built around a public plaza. The Acoma use the first floor of each home for storage and the upper two floors for living. Ladders enable people to climb from one level to another.

Below the mesa, on the valley floor, the Acoma hunted, gathered desert foods, and planted gardens. Men coaxed crops of corn, beans, and squash out of desert soils by planting near springs at the foot of the mesa. Like many desert mesas, theirs holds water in layers of porous sandstone, releasing it slowly to a layer of shale below. The water travels along the nonporous layer of shale until it emerges somewhere at the mesa base. After the Spanish had brought sheep, goats, and horses into the area, men became breeders and herders, but they continued to hunt, especially rabbit and deer.

Acoma men wore buckskin clothing at first and, later, black cotton pants and shirts similar to Spanish

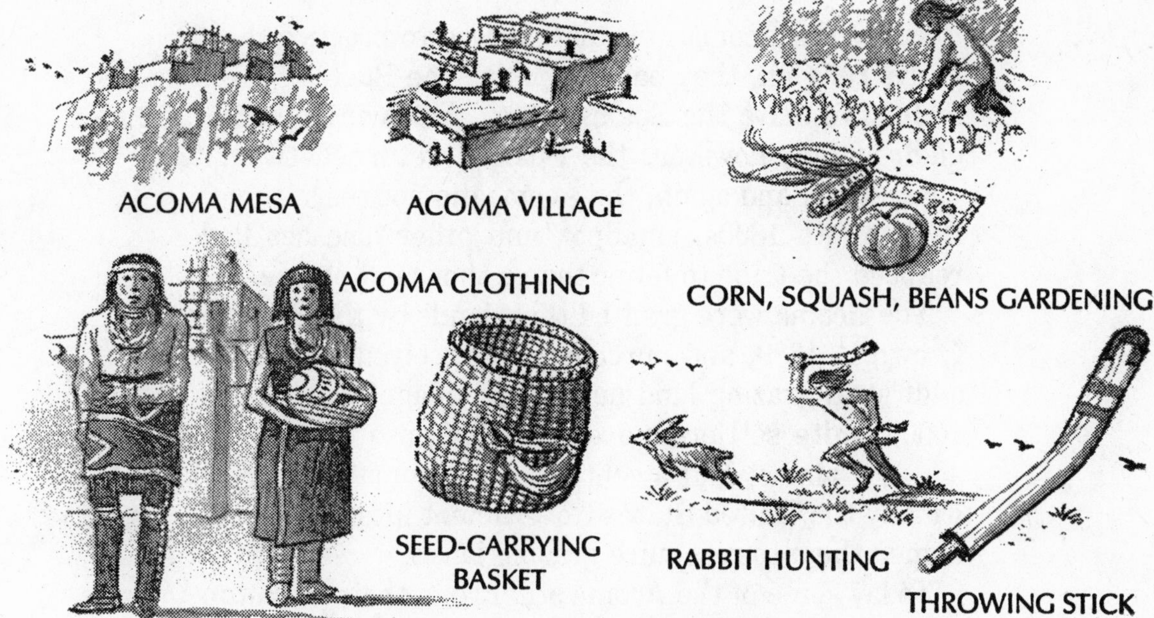

clothing. Women wore moccasins and one-piece dresses that covered one shoulder and tied at the waist.

Each year the Acoma hold festivals—the Rain Dance and the Corn Dance, when they appeal to their gods to bring rain and to thank them for a bountiful harvest. Their most sacred religious ceremonies are conducted underground in chambers called kivas, which are dug deep into the earth and are reachable only by ladder. Kivas are off-limits to non-Indians.

Half of the Acoma died in 1599, when a Spanish explorer came to revenge the death of his brother, who had been killed in the region. When the Spanish returned thirty years later to establish a mission, the Acoma offered no resistance. The Spanish claimed they had come to save the souls of the Indians, but their real purpose was to profit from the sweat of the Acoma. Spanish missionaries worked the Indians very hard to produce crops and handiwork, which the invaders sold in Europe and Mexico at great profit.

Because the Acoma were not allowed to practice their native religion, they eagerly joined the Pueblo Revolt in 1680 to drive the Spanish away. Following a series of droughts, however, the Spanish returned twenty years later, and again, the Acoma did not resist them. By the late 1800s, smallpox and other diseases had reduced the tribe to fewer than a thousand people.

The Acoma were granted their lands by the Spanish Crown in 1689, and purchased or received grants for additional grazing land near their village. During the 1800s white settlers moved illegally onto their lands and, for almost half a century, the Acoma protested. Finally the United States Government intervened and helped them to reacquire grazing lands.

Today some of the Acoma still live in their mesa-top village while others live in communities in the valley below.

ARAPAHO

(eh-RAP-eh-ho)

MEANING OF NAME: He who trades

CULTURE AREA: Plains

LOCATION: Eastern Colorado and southeastern Wyoming

DWELLING TYPE: Tipis

CLOTHING MATERIAL: Skins

TRANSPORTATION: Horses

FOOD: Meat and wild plants

The Arapaho lived near the headwaters of the Platte and Arkansas rivers, which cut deep green swathes through the semiarid land. Juniper, piñon, and cottonwood trees mark the water courses, and tall native grasses fill the surrounding plain. The Arapaho made their homes in the river valleys, which offered shelter, sources of water, and good antelope hunting in winter. In spring when the buffalo came, the Arapaho gathered together on the plains and raised large skin-covered tipis in a circle. Buffalo hunting required everyone's cooperation, and each hunt was preceded by sacred ceremonies and dances of celebration.

Buffalos supplied the Arapaho with everything they needed—food, shelter, clothing, and tools. Women pounded dried buffalo meat together with berries and fat to make pemmican. Hunters carried this nourishing food on trips because it stayed fresh for long periods of time. Women and children gathered berries, nuts, and greens at each campsite. Neighboring tribes called some bands of Arapaho "dog eaters," because they ate dog flesh.

Before horses came to the Plains, dogs pulled family belongings on a small unwheeled cart called a travois. The Arapaho later used horses to pull larger travois.

Men wore buckskin breechcloths, moccasins, and leggings; women wore one-piece sleeveless buckskin dresses. They both wore buffalo-skin robes decorated with quillwork.

The sacred pipe was an important religious symbol used by the Arapaho each year, when they held a celebration called the Sun Dance. The keeper of the pipe, an old man, lived in a painted tipi during the celebration. It took him four nights to tell the story of the tribe's origin, which has never been recorded by a white man.

In the early 1800s some of the tribe moved south and joined the Kiowa and Comanche to fight against bands of Cheyenne. The rest of the tribe went north and joined the Northern Cheyenne, who were fighting against tribes of the Sioux. Eventually they all settled on a reservation in Indian Territory. The Northern Arapaho bands did not like their reservation land and went to live with the Shoshone on their reservation in Wyoming. Those who stayed in Indian territory lost most of their land when their reservation was divided among tribal members and white settlers who wanted to buy land.

Descendants of the Arapaho raise cattle on the Wind River Reservation in Wyoming. Some also live in Oklahoma.

ARIKARA

(eh-REE-keh-reh)

MEANING OF NAME: Horn

CULTURE AREA: Plains

LOCATION: Kansas, South Dakota, and North Dakota

DWELLING TYPES: Earth lodges and tipis

CLOTHING MATERIAL: Skins

TRANSPORTATION: Skin bullboats and snowshoes

FOOD: Corn, meat, and wild foods

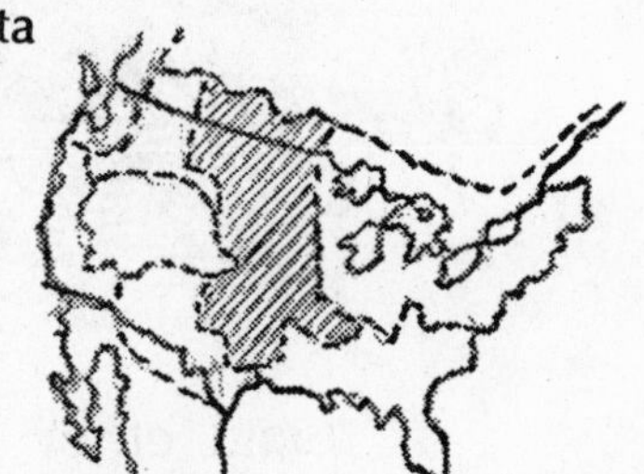

The Arikara lived along the muddy waters of the Missouri River, which flows from the western Rocky Mountains to the eastern edge of the Great Plains. Melting snows and spring rains helped the river to carve steep sandstone bluffs and low fertile valleys across the plains. The Arikara built fortified villages on high bluffs above the river and planted large gardens in the valley below. In the centers of their villages stood large ceremonial lodges which they reserved for festivals and public events. They dug circular floors for their lodges several feet below ground, erected log frames, and covered the frames with branches and heavy sod.

The Arikara, primarily farmers, harvested nine different varieties of corn each year from their fertile valley gardens—enough to use for trade with trappers

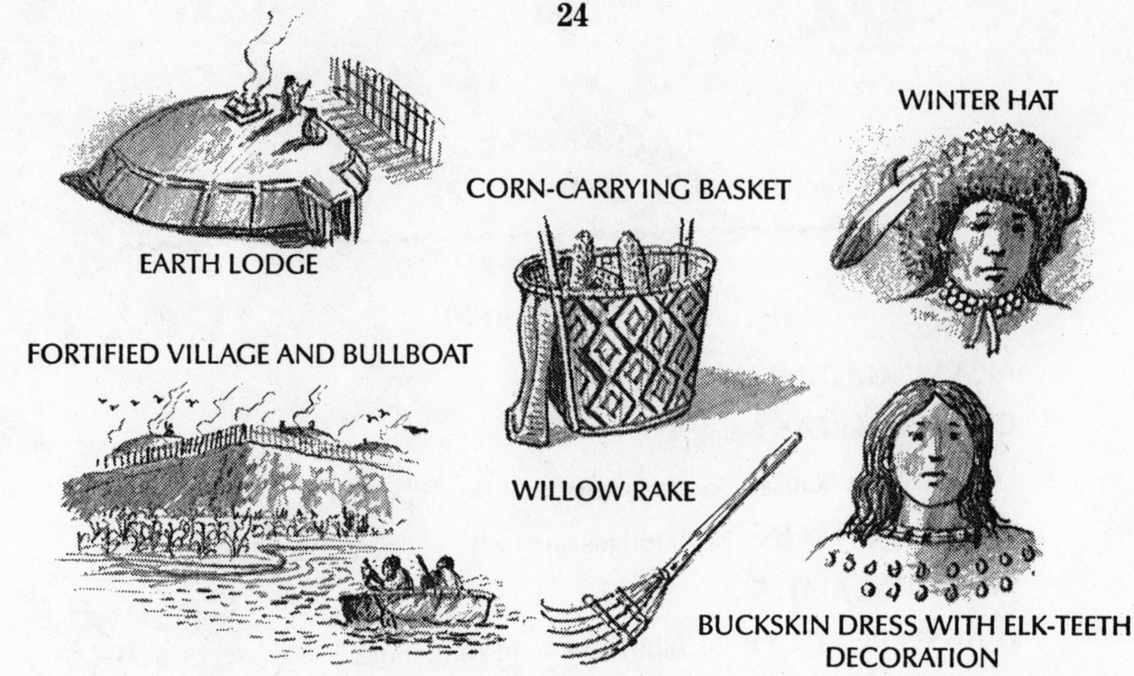

and other tribes. They also raised beans, squash, pumpkins, and sunflowers. In the fall women collected nuts, berries, and wild greens. The men hunted deer, antelope, and buffalo. When hunting, men lived in small skin-covered tipis.

Men swam across swollen rivers and streams steering bullboats filled with women, children, and the family's belongings. Bullboats were made by stretching animal skins over a small round wood frame. In the winter, men traveled over deep snow on finely crafted snowshoes.

The men wore tanned buckskin breechcloths, moccasins, and leggings; the women wore long buckskin dresses. In the wintertime, they both added buffalo-fur robes.

The Arikara, who believe in a supreme spirit that shares its power with lesser spirits, celebrate the planting and harvesting of each new crop by praying, feasting, and dancing.

Many Arikara died from smallpox epidemics in 1789

and 1837. Survivors went to live on a reservation in Nebraska with the Mandan and Hidatsa. When the Homestead Act was passed by Congress in 1862, opening Nebraska to homesteaders, their reservation was reduced considerably in size. Tribal members received small parcels of land and the United States government sold the remaining reservation land to white settlers. In 1950 the U.S. Government built Garrison Dam on Arikara lands and flooded their schools, cemeteries, homes, and their best farmland. The Indians moved to the west side of the new lake, which was formed by the dam, called Lake Sakakawae, where their descendants live today.

ASSINIBOIN
(eh-SIN-eh-boyne)

MEANING OF NAME: One who cooks with heated stones

CULTURE AREA: Plains

LOCATION: Northern Minnesota

DWELLING TYPE: Tipis

CLOTHING MATERIAL: Skins

TRANSPORTATION: Horses, snowshoes, and skin bullboats

FOOD: Meat and wild plants

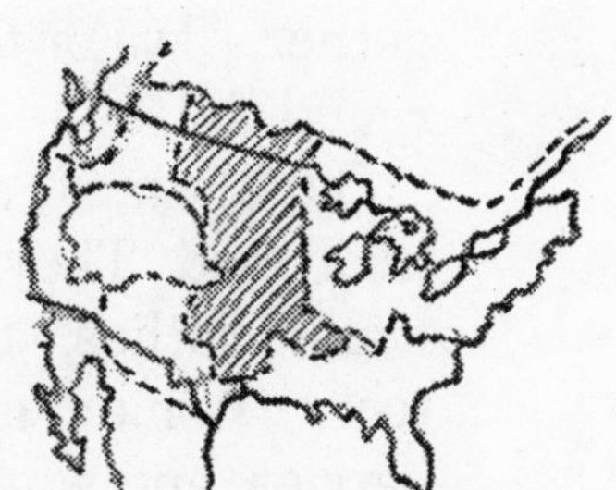

The Assiniboin lived in the dense coniferous forests of the north. Beyond the forests, the land is dotted

with clear blue lakes, streams, and marshes, and is interspersed with rocky hills and low flatlands. Here the Assiniboin hunted deer, elk, antelope, and bighorn sheep in winter. In spring they gathered on the treeless plains to organize the annual buffalo hunt. Buffalo hunting was a communal activity in which many men participated. They celebrated sacred ceremonies before each hunt and carefully planned their strategies. Families set up large skin-covered tipis in circles—sometimes as many as two hundred clustered together. Two or three families shared each thirty-foot-round tipi.

Buffalo meat supplied the Assiniboin with most of their food. They used the remainder of the animal to make clothes, tipi covers, household utensils, and tools. Women made pemmican and gathered nuts, berries, and wild roots at each new campsite.

Men wore tanned buckskin breechcloths, moccasins, and leggings; women wore long buckskin dresses. In cold weather they added buffalo-fur robes.

The chief god of the Assiniboin is named Wakan

Tanka. The Assiniboin believe that everyone has four souls: three souls die with the body, and one is retained in the form of a spirit bundle, to which friends bring gifts until the spirit is released.

At the time of European contact, the Assiniboin were a very large and powerful tribe. By 1858, however, four thousand of their people were dead, the result of smallpox contracted through trading with the Europeans. The survivors were forced to cede their lands and move to a reservation in western Montana. The government did not supply them with the food promised, and hundreds of Indians starved to death. Later their reservation land was divided among tribal members and white settlers who bought the land from the government.

Descendants of the Assiniboin live on reservations in Montana and in Canada.

BELLA COOLA

(bel-eh-KOOL-eh)

MEANING OF NAME: Unknown

CULTURE AREA: Northwest

LOCATION: British Columbia, Canada

DWELLING TYPE: Plank houses

CLOTHING MATERIAL: Cedar bark

TRANSPORTATION: Cedar dugout canoes

FOOD: Fish, meat, and wild plants

The Bella Coola lived along the icy blue waters of the Bella Coola River, which rushes down from the mighty Rocky Mountains and crashes into the waters of the Pacific Ocean. Off the coast, the warm waters of the Japan Current brush the shoreline, producing rainy mild temperatures the year round. At the mouth of the Bella Coola River, where it flares out to meet the sea, the Indians built a permanent village of peak-roofed houses framed with logs and covered with cedar planks. Many houses had front doorways flanked with handsome cedar posts carved with figures representing the clan.

The Bella Coola depended upon salmon as their main food source. Several times each year thousands of salmon spawned upriver, and each time, the Bella Coola waited with their expertly placed nets. Besides salmon, they netted quantities of candlefish, which yielded a valuable oil. They traded the oil to inland tribes for furs and buckskins. To supplement their diet, women collected berries and roots in the mountains. Men hunted bears and porcupines inland, and seals, ducks, and geese along the coast.

The Bella Coola traveled in large ocean-going dugout canoes, usually painted black with white fish designs.

Men often wore no clothes, but women wore woven cedar-bark skirts. They all wore cedar-bark capes and blankets made waterproof with a thin coating of oil. Cedar bark was often woven into several layers for extra warmth.

The Bella Coola believe that in the wintertime supernatural beings who haunt the world return to their real homes in the sky. The Bella Coola entertain these Sky-Gods by hosting parties, dancing, and wearing

masks. Many years ago, these parties, called potlatches, lasted several days and often celebrated an important event—a birth, a name-giving, an initiation ceremony, a marriage, or a death. Each host tried to outdo the others by giving away bigger and better gifts to his guests. Gifts of copper, shell, and woven blankets were important indicators of wealth and status. The richest and most important clans and groups, of course, gave the largest number of potlatches.

Between 1793 and 1894 the Bella Coola were visited by European explorers, a Methodist missionary, gold diggers, Hudson Bay Company fur trappers, and Norwegian colonists. By the time the American loggers moved into their region, large numbers of the Bella Coola suffered from severe alcoholism and many others had died from European diseases.

Descendants of the Bella Coola now live on a reservation in British Columbia.

BLACKFOOT

(BLAK-FOOT)

MEANING OF NAME: Moccasins which became black from prairie-fire ash

CULTURE AREA: Plains

LOCATION: Northern Montana and southern Alberta, Canada

DWELLING TYPE: Tipis

CLOTHING MATERIAL: Skins

TRANSPORTATION: Horses

FOOD: Meat and wild plants

The Blackfoot lived in a region of tall mountains and swiftly flowing rivers that tumble out of the Rocky Mountains in all directions. Many bands of the Blackfoot sought winter shelter along the Flathead River, which begins in British Columbia and flows into and through the clear waters of Flathead Lake in northern Montana. They hunted deer, elk, moose, antelope, and bear along the river in winter. In spring they moved onto the open plains where they spent the rest of the year tracking migrating herds of buffalo. The Blackfoot built very large and distinctive tipis—framing poles extended four to six feet above the top of the skin cover. Their tipis were set in circles so that their

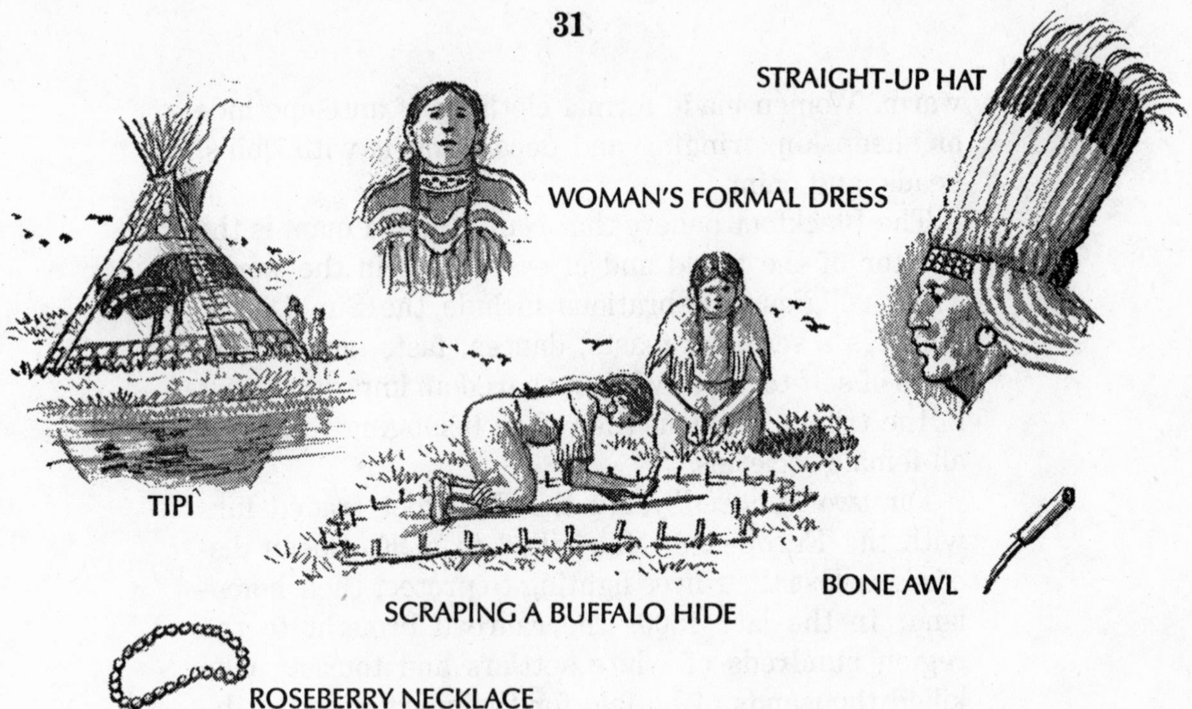

warriors could meet in the center to organize the hunt and conduct sacred rituals. When the buffalo came, the hunters surrounded them wearing animal disguises, driving them into enclosures where they were easy to shoot.

Buffalos supplied the Blackfoot with most of their food, clothing, shelter, and household tools. The women dried and preserved the meat and made some of it into pemmican. Hunters often used pemmican to trade with European trappers. The Blackfoot women and children gathered berries, nuts, and wild foods wherever they camped.

Men wore long buckskin leggings that passed under a narrow belt at the waist and hung down in front; women wore full-length, one-piece sleeveless dresses tied at their shoulders. In cold weather they added sleeves to their dresses. Everyone wore buffalo-skin robes in winter. Their moccasins were made of buffalo skin with the fur left on the inside to make them warm. Women made formal clothing of antelope hide or sheepskin, fringing and decorating it with quills, beads, and paint.

The Blackfoot believe that Napi, the old man, is the creator of the world and of everything in the world. Their religious celebrations include the Sun Dance, which is a series of feasts, dances, fasts, and exhibitions of self-torture. Women shared an important part in the tribe's religious life, often belonging to special all-female societies.

For two hundred years the Blackfoot traded furs with the Europeans. Many died from European diseases or lost their lives fighting to protect their homeland. In the late 1800s the railroad brought to the region hundreds of white settlers and tourists who killed thousands of buffalo for the sport of it. In the winter of 1883, eight hundred Blackfoot Indians died from starvation because there were no buffalo left to hunt. Survivors ceded their land and moved to reservations in Canada and Montana. The United States government gave them money, cattle, and farm supplies in exchange.

Descendants of the Blackfoot live on reservations in Alberta, Canada, and in northwestern Montana, where they are successful cattle ranchers and farmers.

CADDO
(KAD-do)

MEANING OF NAME: Chief

CULTURE AREA: Southeast

LOCATION: Louisiana, Arkansas, and eastern Texas

DWELLING TYPE: Earth lodges

CLOTHING MATERIALS: Skins and fiber

TRANSPORTATION: Wooden dugout canoes, cane rafts, and horses

FOOD: Corn, meat, and wild plants

The Caddo Indians lived in the broad valley of the Red River, which flows through the state of Louisiana and empties into the Gulf of New Mexico. It is a valley filled with rich fertile soil and blessed with warm year-round temperatures. The Caddo raised two bountiful crops each year of corn, beans, and squash in their valley. They built permanent villages and placed their houses in a large circle around an open area reserved for games, rituals, dancing, and music-making. They preferred to dig the floors of their round log-framed houses several feet below the ground. They covered them with branches and heavy sod. Several extended families lived in each house.

The Caddo dried large quantities of corn and stored it away for winter. When all the crops were harvested in the fall, the men went deer hunting, wearing stuffed

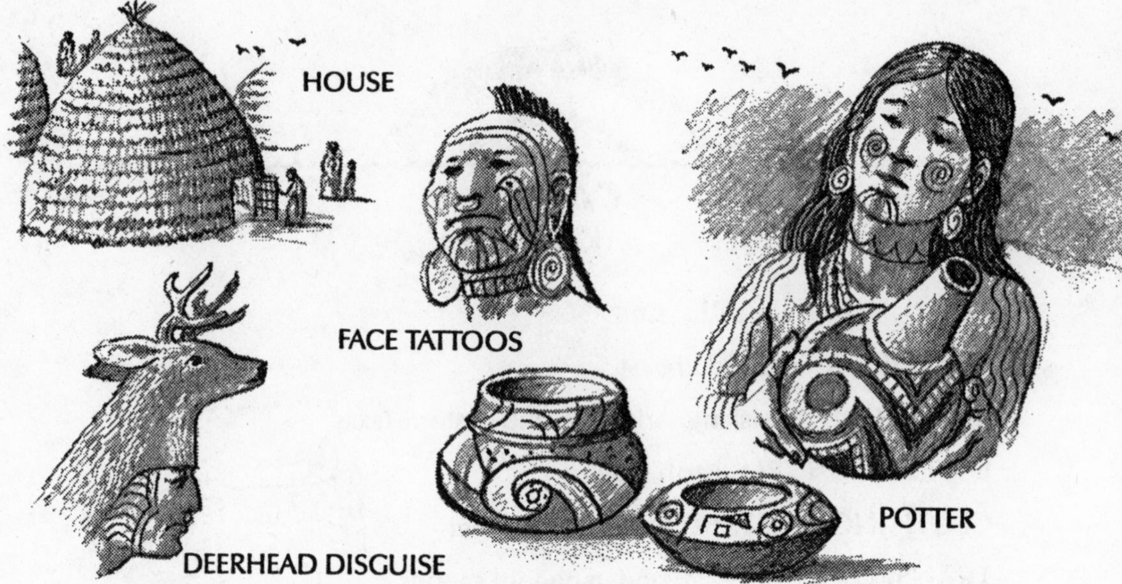

deer-head disguises, and the women and children left the villages to gather berries and nuts.

Men wore buckskin breechcloths; women wore short skirts of woven mulberry bark. In colder weather, they added fur robes. The Caddo decorated their entire bodies with elaborate tattoos of animal, bird, and floral designs. Body paint, as well as body tattooing, was popular with many tribes who wanted to supplement their colorful clothing. Tattoos were scratched onto the body using sharp implements of stone, shell, and bone and were made colorful by rubbing charcoal and vegetable dyes into the scratches.

The Caddo worship the sun and a number of lesser spirits. Each year they pray, dance, and make music to celebrate the planting and harvesting of their crops.

In the 1700s the French and Spanish fought against each other using Caddo villages as defense posts. Outbreaks of smallpox and measles soon spread through the tribe, killing many of its members. The survivors were forced to cede their lands and move to Texas, from where they were later driven. They finally moved to a reservation in Indian Territory. Later their reservation lands were divided up—the Indians received individual parcels and white settlers bought the rest.

Descendants of the Caddo live in Oklahoma.

CAHUILLA
(keh-WEEYUH)

MEANING OF NAME: Master boss

CULTURE AREA: California

LOCATION: Southern California

DWELLING TYPE: Round, brush-covered, domed houses

CLOTHING MATERIALS: Skins and fibers

TRANSPORTATION: Unknown

FOOD: Meat, fish, and wild plants

The Cahuilla lived in a rich, warm valley interspersed with rocky canyons and desert that stretched from the San Bernardino Mountains south to the tip of the Salton Sea. The amount and variety of wild food was so vast that they lived off the land all year round. As soon as one food source was diminished, another became available. They lived in groups in sheltered canyons near sources of water. They built long, nar-

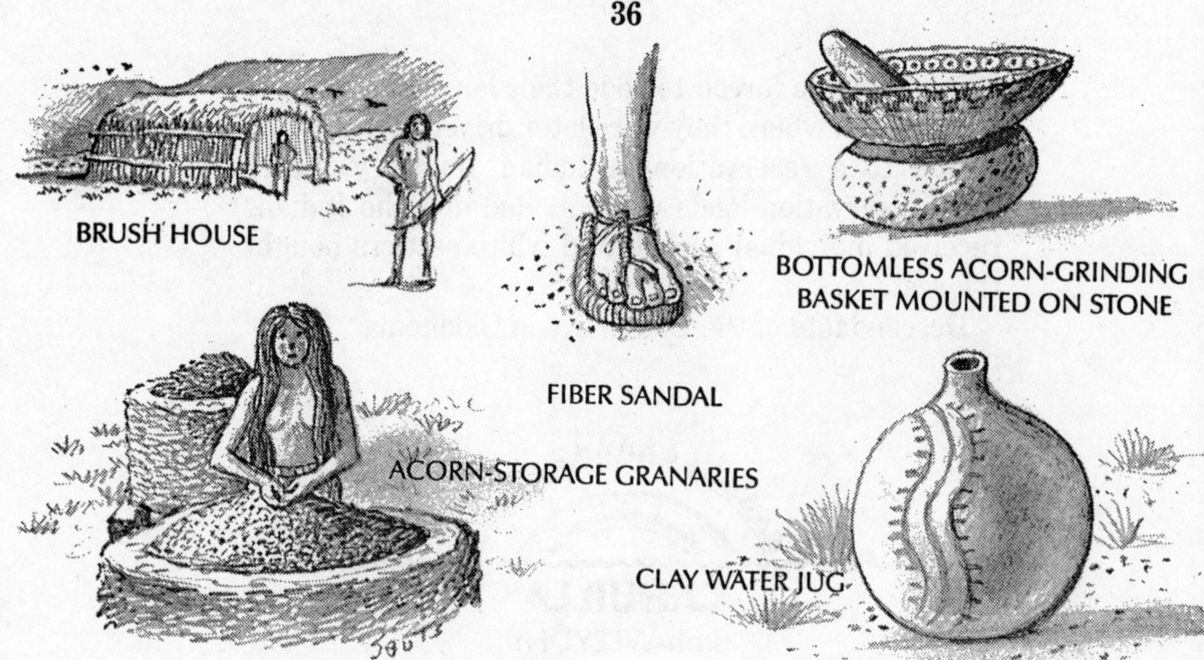

row dome-shaped houses with straight sides covered with brush. The largest house belonged to the chief. Each major village had a centrally located ceremonial house and common land that was shared by all the villagers. Additional land was assigned to clans, families, or individuals. The Cahuilla connected their villages with well-worn paths, many of them marked with clan drawings scratched onto rocks.

Clans living in the mountains spent most of their time hunting elk and deer, while those living in the foothills hunted, trapped, snared, and netted rabbits and other small animals. They all collected large crops of acorns each year and the women and children gathered many seeds, berries, roots, and wild greens.

Men wore buckskin breechcloths; women wore two-sided buckskin or woven-fiber aprons. They covered their feet with tough pieces of leather or with fiber sandals, which they strapped on with buckskin thongs.

The Cahuilla believe soul spirits live on after a

person dies. They employed shamans to call on the supernatural powers, and women doctors cured sicknesses using herbal concoctions.

The Cahuilla had very little contact with Europeans until the late 1800s. Many of the tribe then died from smallpox epidemics, and the survivors were forced to live on a closely supervised reservation in California. Government officials invited white school teachers and missionaries to live on the reservation, and they outlawed the practice of the native religion. The government neglected to help the Cahuilla when neighboring settlers diverted their streams and took away their water, making it impossible for them to raise crops.

Descendants of the Cahuilla live on a small reservation in southern California where they are trying to return to their traditional lifestyle.

CATAWBA

(keh-TAW-beh)

MEANING OF NAME: People of the river

CULTURE AREA: Southeast

LOCATION: Central South Carolina

DWELLING TYPE: Bark-covered houses

CLOTHING MATERIAL: Skins

TRANSPORTATION: Unknown

FOOD: Corn, meat, fish, and wild foods

The Catawba lived in the fertile valleys of the Wateree and Santee rivers, which run from the foothills of the Blue Ridge Mountains to the Atlantic Coast. Deer, elk, and bear roamed the dense hardwood forests to the north, while grapes, blackberries, and many nuts and berries covered the foothills. Along the humid, junglelike coast, warm sandy beaches nourished a variety of succulent shellfish, and palmetto and live oak trees provided food and an unending source of building material for the Catawba. The rich soils, mild year-round temperatures, and abundant rainfall between the mountains and the coast enabled the Catawba to raise large crops. They built square, bark-covered houses and arranged them around a central square. In the middle of the square they built a public house or temple, reserving it for ceremonies and special events.

Large plantings of corn, beans, squash, and gourds supplied the tribe with most of its food. The gourds were not eaten but their tough, lightweight shells provided bowls, cups, and scoops.

The men wore deerskin breechcloths and the women wore short deerskin skirts. They both added fur capes, leggings, and moccasins in colder weather.

The Catawba believe that all living things come from the sky and that good and bad spirits live in both the natural and the supernatural world.

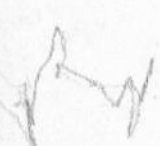

Catawba villages were situated along a well-traveled Indian trail used by British fur trappers. The Catawba joined the fur trade because they wanted European trade goods. To protect their trapping territory, however, they fought against bands of the Shawnee, Iroquois, and Cherokee, who killed many of their people. The Catawba adopted members of other tribes to make up for their losses in battles and from smallpox epidemics.

In 1840 some of the Catawba signed a treaty exchanging their lands in South Carolina for land in North Carolina. The settlers in North Carolina, however, refused to honor the treaty, so the Catawba were left homeless until officials gave them a tiny strip of barren land on the west bank of the Catawba River.

Descendants of the Catawba live on a state reservation in South Carolina.

CAYUGA

(kah-YOOGUH)

MEANING OF NAME: Where the boats were taken out; also Mucky land

CULTURE AREA: Northeast

LOCATION: West central New York

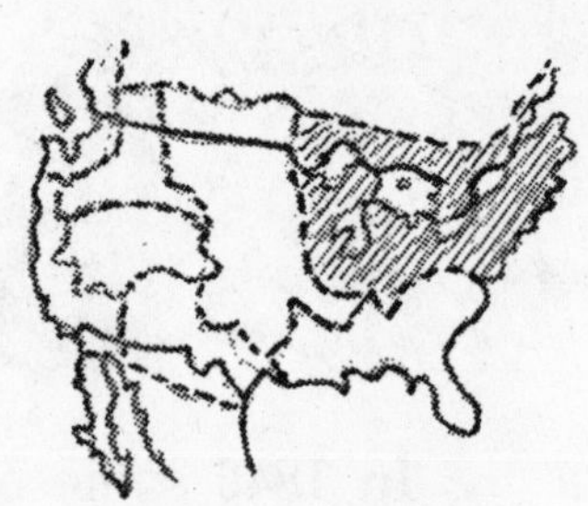

DWELLING TYPE: Longhouses

CLOTHING MATERIAL: Skins

TRANSPORTATION: Elm-bark canoes

FOOD: Corn, meat, and wild plants

The Cayuga lived along the steep shores of Cayuga and Owasco lakes, in central New York State. The land surrounding the lakes is good for farming, and the fields and wooded hills offer abundant game, berries, and wild greens. Yet the Cayuga did not farm the land as their neighbors did. Instead, they spent all year hunting, fishing, and gathering wild foods. They built barrel-shaped, multifamily longhouses by placing two rows of saplings in the ground, bending them at the top, and tying them together. Elm bark was the most available material to cover their Iroquois-style longhouses, but when it was not available they used the bark of other trees.

In the spring Cayuga families camped in the maple tree groves, where they collected maple sap. They boiled it down into syrup and sugar and wrapped it

into strips of bark for use all year. When the men left the village to go hunting, the women and children gathered wild plants near their villages.

The men wore deerskin breechcloths; the women wore short deerskin skirts. They both wore moccasins and warm deerskin capes in cold weather.

Every January the Cayuga carry on an eight-day celebration during which the False Face Society participates in healing exercises. Its members wear grotesque, wooden masks that depict spirits seen in the forests and in people's dreams. The masks themselves are said to be very powerful and must have tobacco burned for them from time to time. They also must be kept out of closed, dark places. Society members who wear the masks have special powers and can handle hot coals without getting burned.

The Cayuga belonged to the League of Six Nations, sometimes called the Iroquois Confederacy. League members, who include the Seneca, Onondaga, Oneida,

Mohawk, and Tuscarora, refer to the Cayuga as "younger brothers." The League, founded between A.D. 1400 and 1600 by a Huron mystic named Deganawida, and his disciple, Hiawatha, was organized to stop intertribal warfare. A council of great chiefs, chosen from members of the five original tribes, drew up laws and decided upon customs, which would be maintained by League members. The Revolutionary War permanently divided the tribes, and after the war the council chiefs voted to extinguish the council fires, ending a powerful and united Iroquois Confederacy.

Throughout the 1600s and 1700s, members of the Iroquois Confederacy fought against the French and neighboring tribes in an effort to control the fur trade. They tried to remain neutral during the American Revolution, but the British convinced them to fight with them. After the war, American soldiers burned Cayuga villages to the ground.

In 1789 some of the Cayuga signed a treaty with New York State officials ceding their land in exchange for an annual payment of money. They moved to the Seneca reservation in western New York State and to Canada, but they never received the money promised them. Many years later the State of New York made two payments to the Cayuga, then stopped. State officials refuse to make the remaining payments because they claim the Cayuga live on a reservation that belongs to another tribe, or else live outside the country (in Canada). The Cayuga do not see this as a problem and continue to petition New York State's courts for their money.

Descendants of the Cayuga live in New York and Canada.

CHEROKEE

(CHER-eh-kee)

MEANING OF NAME: The real, or principal, people

CULTURE AREA: Southeast

LOCATION: Northern Georgia, eastern Tennessee, and western North Carolina

DWELLING TYPE: Mat-covered houses

CLOTHING MATERIAL: Skins

TRANSPORTATION: Wooden dugout canoes

FOOD: Corn, meat, fish, and wild plants

The Cherokee lived in the rugged southern Allegheny and Great Smokey mountains. In the nearby foothills, deer, bear, elk, turkey, and other animals came to feed on the dense hemlock, pine, and balsam forests. Freshwater streams tumbled out of the mountains and stretched across the fertile flatlands, providing abundant fish. The Cherokee situated their small villages along inland rivers and streams and built their homes from wooden poles covered inside and out with woven mats. They arranged them around a central Council House, which they reserved for religious ceremonies and festivities. The Council House had a conical thatched roof, a floor dug below ground, and sides of woven cane and grass.

Women raised corn, beans, squash, and sunflowers, which they harvested in the fall and preserved for the winter. They raised gourds, and used the shells for cups, bowls, and containers. With their children, women gathered quantities of wild grapes, blackberries, huckleberries, nuts, and greens. The men often built stone weirs in streams to trap fish. Sometimes they put a poisonous mixture of roots and bark into the water to make the fish groggy and easy to catch by hand.

Men wore deerskin breechcloths; women wore short deerskin skirts. When it was cold, both sexes wore fur robes and long shawls tied over the left shoulder. Men wore high deerskin boots with moccasin-style bottoms, especially when hunting.

The Cherokee believe in a spiritual creator and in spirits who inhabit the Sun, Moon, and stars. They dance, pray, and feast each August at a festival called the Green Corn Dance, giving thanks to the spirits to insure a bountiful harvest.

A Cherokee man named Sequoyah developed a way to write in the Cherokee language using a native alphabet. In 1828 this alphabet was used at New Echota, Georgia, to print the first Native American newspaper. The newspaper's editor was an educated Cherokee named Elias Boudinot, who printed the news in both English and Cherokee. Publication of the paper ceased in 1835 when the Cherokee were forcibly moved to Indian Territory.

In 1785 the Cherokee signed a treaty with the young American government that guaranteed their independence as a nation. They later fought with General Andrew Jackson at the Battle of Horseshoe Bend, helping his soldiers defeat the Creeks. A Cherokee soldier saved Jackson's life during the battle, but when Jackson became president of the United States, he turned his back when Georgian settlers moved

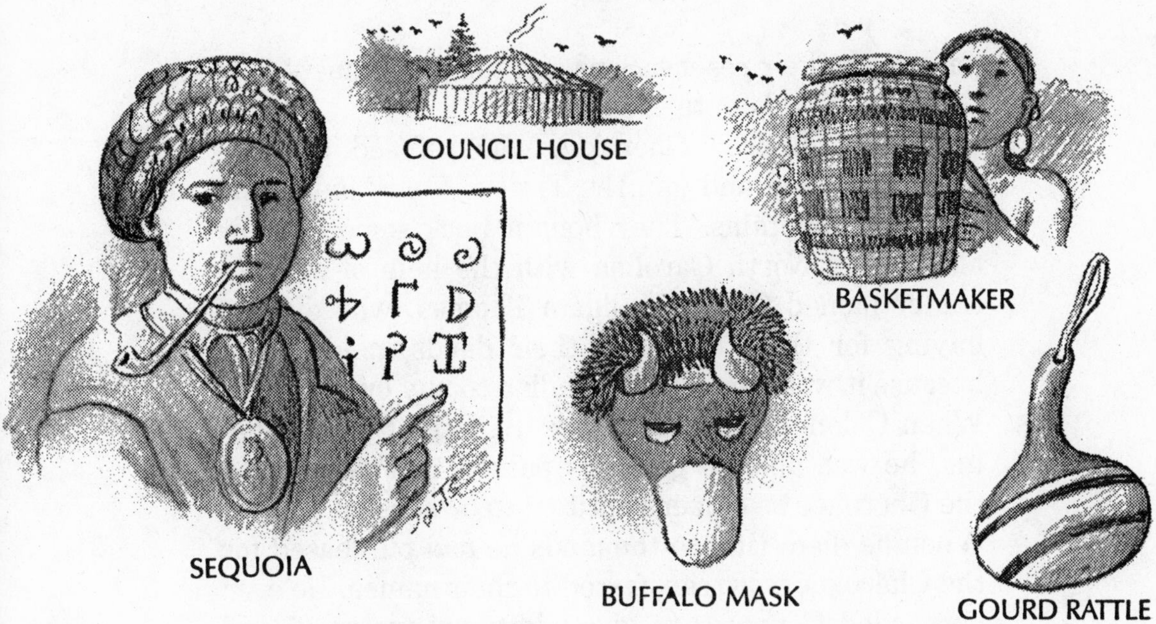

COUNCIL HOUSE

BASKETMAKER

SEQUOIA

BUFFALO MASK

GOURD RATTLE

illegally onto Cherokee lands. He also introduced into Congress the Indian Removal Act of 1830, which forced the removal of all eastern Indian tribes to west of the Mississippi River. The Cherokee fought their case in court and, in 1832, the Supreme Court decided in their favor. But President Jackson ignored the court's decision. He ordered government troops to forcibly march sixteen hundred of the Cherokee westward, a trip known as "The Trail of Tears," which cost the lives of almost five hundred of them along the way. In spite of their pain and hardship, the survivors prospered in the new land. They became one of the Five Civilized Tribes, which included the Chickasaw, Choctaw, Creek, and Seminole, who adopted a democratic form of government with a constitution, courts, and regular elections. When Oklahoma sought statehood in 1907, white settlers there wanted the Indian land and forced the United States government to divide reservation lands. Tribal members were given parcels on their reservations and the government sold the remaining land to the settlers.

Fifteen hundred Cherokee who refused to leave their homeland and join the Trail of Tears hid in the Smokey Mountains. They bought back some of their old land in North Carolina with the help of a white trader named Colonel William Thomas, who did the buying for them and held their deeds in his name because it was illegal for an Indian to buy or own land. When Colonel Thomas became a United States senator, he was able to get laws passed that recognized the Cherokee as citizens entitled to ownership of land. When he died, title to the lands he had purchased for the Cherokee was transferred to their names. He even persuaded Congress to give additional tracts of land to the Cherokee. These land parcels are part of the present-day Cherokee Indian reservation.

Descendants of the Cherokee live on their reservations in North Carolina and in Oklahoma.

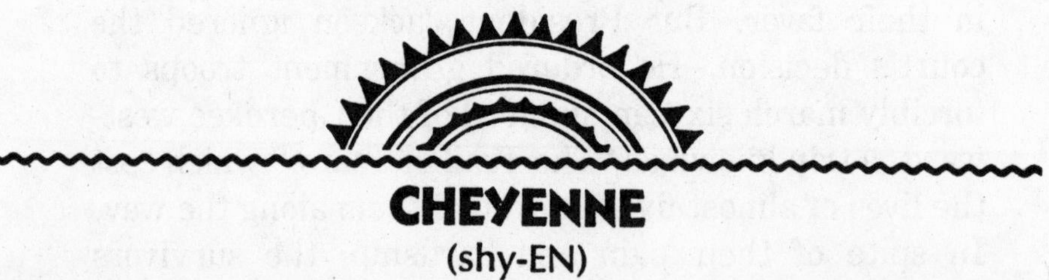

CHEYENNE

(shy-EN)

MEANING OF NAME: People of strange speech

CULTURE AREA: Plains

LOCATION: North Dakota

DWELLING TYPE: Tipis

CLOTHING MATERIAL: Skins

TRANSPORTATION: Horses

FOOD: Meat and wild plants

The Cheyenne lived in a region of fertile river valleys, prairies, wooded hills, lakes, and buttes. The waters of the mighty Missouri River supported healthy stands of cottonwood and willow, and, on the surrounding plains, prairie grass formed thick mats. In the east along the Red River, poplars, box elder, elm, and birch marked the river's edge, and highbush cranberries, chokecherries, grapes, and plums grew along its banks. Animals roamed over the entire region, especially buffalo, which came to feed on the luxuriant grass. In the winter small bands of the Cheyenne set up their tipis in sheltered valleys near good sources of water, but the rest of the year, on horseback, they tracked the herds of restless buffalo. The Cheyenne set up their tipis in well-organized circles each time they stopped to hunt. The men conducted sacred rituals and plotted ways to outwit their prey.

Buffalo meat supplied the Cheyenne with most of their food, and they used the remainder of the animal for clothes, tipi coverings, and household tools. Wherever the band made camp, the women and children collected berries, nuts, and wild greens, especially turnip greens.

The men wore buckskin breechcloths, moccasins, and shirts; the women wore one-piece dresses and moccasins decorated with quills. They added leggings and robes of buffalo skin in cold weather.

The Cheyenne believe in Heammawehio, the creator

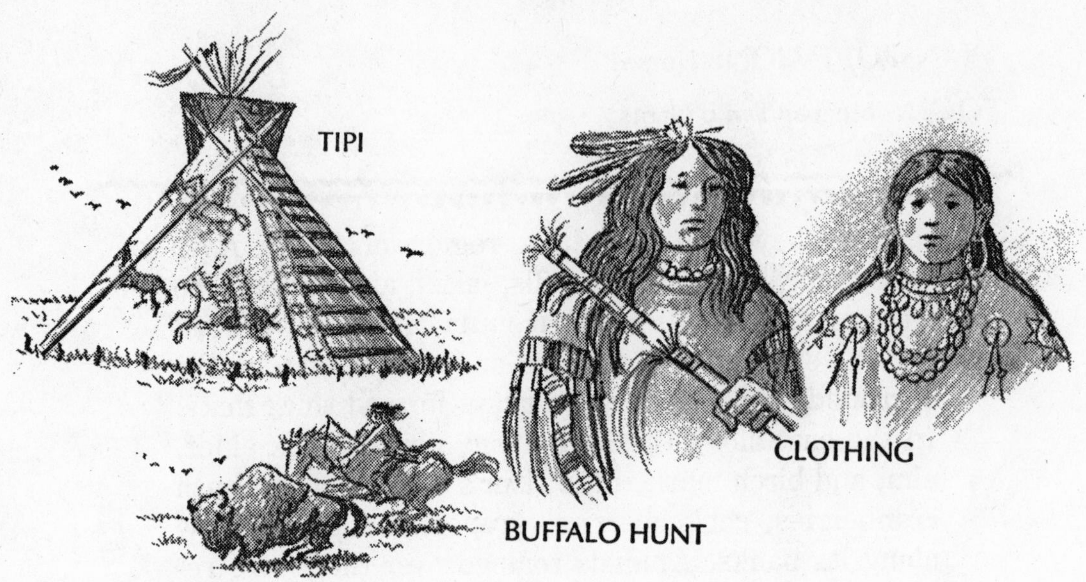

of all things, who lives in the sky. They also believe in their hero, Sweet Medicine, who gave them four arrows—two with power over men, and two with power over the buffalo.

The resourceful Cheyenne once lived in bark-covered wigwams and gathered wild rice in the northern woodlands. Then they moved south, became full-time farmers, and built earth lodges. By the 1700s they were expert buffalo hunters and lived in tipis on the plains. The Gold Rush brought miners and white settlers seeking land into their territory, but the Cheyenne refused to sell. United States troops went to war over the land, and when Chief Black Kettle and two hundred of his people finally surrendered under a flag of truce, frightened troops massacred them all. This angered the Cheyenne and their friends, the Arapaho, who banded together to raid white settlements. The raiding and fighting lasted ten years and is known as the Sioux Wars.

The Northern Cheyenne eventually went to live on

a reservation in Indian Territory, which was too crowded, had no hunting, and had soil too poor to support crops. When they did not receive the supplies they had been promised, Dull Knife, a leader in the Sioux Wars, and a group of his followers left the reservation to hunt. Troops tracked them down and killed all but a few who hid in the mountains. In the end, only eighty Cheyenne survivors went to live on a reservation in southeastern Montana.

Descendants of the Cheyenne live in Oklahoma and Montana.

CHICKASAW

(CHIK-eh-saw)

MEANING OF NAME: Unknown

CULTURE AREA: Southeast

LOCATION: Northern Mississippi

DWELLING TYPE: Earth lodges

CLOTHING MATERIAL: Skins

TRANSPORTATION: Bald cypress, poplar, and pine dugout canoes

FOOD: Corn, meat, fish, and wild plants

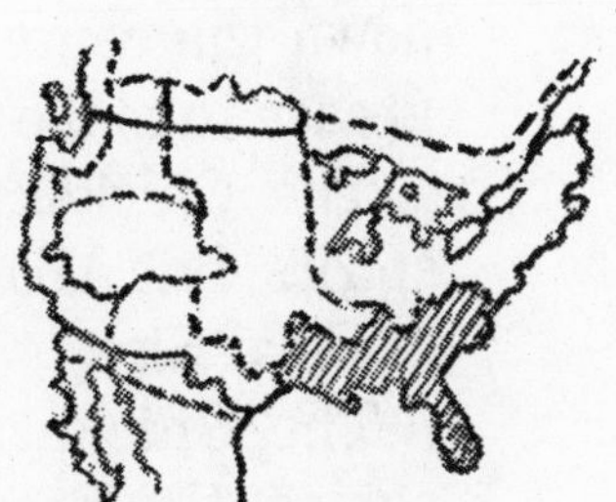

The Chickasaw lived between the mighty Mississippi and Tombigbee rivers on rich, rolling, black prairie land. Men hunted along the wooded Pontotoc Ridge, where deer and bear came to feed and rest.

They prized the bearskins and the grease they obtained by capturing hibernating bears in their dens. The Chickasaw built large round houses—sometimes 25 feet in diameter—with the foundations dug several feet into the ground. They framed their houses with logs and covered them with woven cane and thick layers of clay. They arranged them in a semicircle, leaving an open area for public meetings, ceremonies, and games. Several extended families lived in each house. In the summer some families preferred to live by themselves in small thatched-roof houses covered with mats or bark.

Warm temperatures and plenty of rain made the growing season especially long, and Chickasaw women planted large gardens of corn, beans, and squash each year. Men fished in the rivers, often poisoning the water with a concoction of roots and bark to drug the fish and make them easier to catch.

Men wore simple deerskin breechcloths and shirts, and women wore finely tanned deerskin dresses. In the wintertime, they both added heavy bearskin robes and high deerskin boots. Sometimes the men shaved their heads, leaving a long strip of hair called a "roach" down the center. They soaked their roaches in bear grease to make them stand up straight.

The Chickasaw believe in many witches and evil spirits, but Aboninite is their primary god and he lives in Clear Sky.

The Chickasaw, allied with the British, fought against the French and won. They often adopted survivors from other tribes to make up for their own battle losses. Englishmen married Chickasaw women, and their half-breed children inherited the clan status of their mother and the English prominence of their father. They functioned comfortably in both worlds.

COUNCIL HOUSE, c. 1890

CHICKASAW SEAL

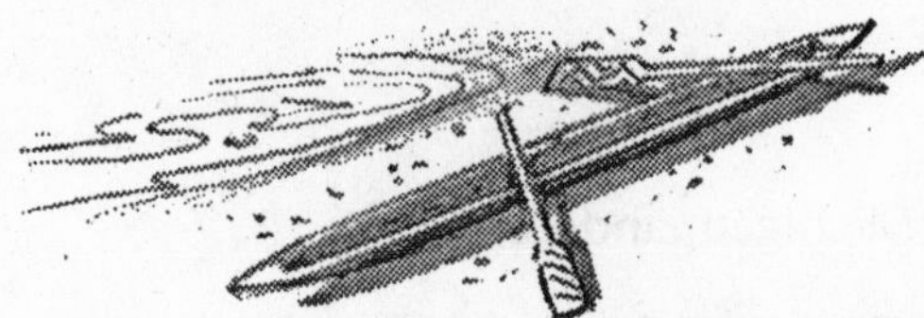

DUGOUT CANOE

CHICKASAW GOVERNOR, c. 1890

A number of wealthy Chickasaw owned huge plantations and kept over a thousand Black slaves. After the Indian Removal Act was passed in 1830 and all Indians were ordered west of the Mississippi, the Chickasaw surrendered their plantations, ceded their lands, and moved to Indian Territory. They took their slaves with them and purchased land from the Choctaw, who were already living on a reservation. They built sawmills and blacksmith shops, created prosperous farms, and sent their children to European-style schools. As a member of the Five Civilized Tribes, they had a democratic form of government including a constitution, courts, and regular elections. Their prosperity was ignored, however, when Oklahoma obtained statehood in 1907 and the Indian government was dissolved. Their reservation land was reduced in size—tribal members received parcels of land and white settlers bought the remaining land.

Descendants of the Chickasaw live in Oklahoma and Mississippi.

CHIPPEWA or OJIBWA

(CHIP-eh-waw) or (ow-JIB-waw)

MEANING OF NAME: Puckered up

CULTURE AREA: Northeast

LOCATION: Wisconsin, Minnesota, Michigan, and Canada

DWELLING TYPES: Bark- or mat-covered wigwams

CLOTHING MATERIAL: Skins

TRANSPORTATION: Snowshoes and birch-bark canoes

FOOD: Wild rice, meat, fish, and wild plants

The Chippewa lived west of the Great Lakes on a broad rolling plain carved out of the mountains long ago by four great glaciers. In the north, the old Laurentian highlands give birth to several mighty rivers, which flow in different directions. The area is plagued with severe winds, long, cold winters and little rainfall in the summer. It is also above the climate line for growing Indian corn, so tribes of the Chippewa could not depend upon harvesting cultivated crops. Instead they traveled all year in large bands of related clansmen—gathering wild plants, hunting, and fishing. In their villages they built large, round dome-shaped wigwams framed with thick saplings and covered with bark or mats sewed of cattail leaves. In each wigwam eight family members lived together.

When the men were hunting, they built small wooden lodges with peaked roofs for themselves.

The Chippewa spent several weeks gathering and preserving wild rice, which supplied them with most of their food. They collected it from freshwater marshes. The men paddled lightweight canoes through the shallow water and the women and children gently knocked the rice kernels off their stalks into the canoe. Sometimes the women planted small gardens of corn, beans, and squash, but the growing season was very short, so they often harvested crops before they were ripe. In spring, many families camped in the maple tree groves and collected sap, which they boiled down into syrup and sugar. Chippewa women did most of the freshwater fishing except in winter, when the men speared fish through the ice. Some families moved to favorite duck-hunting sites in the fall or hunted and trapped deer, bear, moose, and small animals to provide themselves with meat.

Men wore quill-decorated buckskin breechcloths; women wore sleeveless deerskin dresses belted at the waist and tied over one shoulder. Sometimes they wore underclothing woven of plant fibers. Everyone wore leggings and moccasins, heavy fur robes, and cone-shaped leather caps and mittens in cold weather. They also wore coats woven of rabbit skins, and they insulated their moccasins with rabbit fur.

The Chippewa believe that spirits control natural events, are responsible for people's health, and lure game to the hunter's trap. Their primary spirit, Manitou, inhabits trees, birds, animals, and the sky. He likes tobacco, which he gets through offerings of ground-up leaves and pipe smoke. Myths tell about Wenebajo, the good-guy trickster who taught the people about corn, tobacco, and medicinal plants.

MAT-COVERED WIGWAM
MAN'S HAT, c. 1800
WOMAN'S LEGGING
WILD-RICE GATHERING
CEREMONIAL PIPE

French trappers, missionaries, and tribes of the Iroquois forced many of the Chippewa to move south or west, where they adopted a Plains lifestyle. Later they were forcibly moved onto reservations. When valuable minerals were discovered in 1854 on one of their reservations, government officials offered to buy the land, and the Chippewa agreed to sell so that they could buy back some of their old homeland. Some bands of the Chippewa continue to fight in the United States courts today for their land, much of which was taken for nonpayment of taxes many years ago. They maintain that their original treaty specified that there would be no taxes levied against them and therefore the land is still theirs. At present they are seeking the return of one hundred acres in Minnesota.

Descendants of the Chippewa live in Canada, and in the United States in Oklahoma, North Dakota, Montana, and a number of urban areas in other states.

CHITAMACHA

(chit-teh-MA-kah)

MEANING OF NAME: They have cooking vessels

CULTURE AREA: Southeast

LOCATION: Louisiana

DWELLING TYPE: Thatched houses

CLOTHING MATERIAL: Fiber

TRANSPORTATION: Pine and cedar dugout canoes

FOOD: Corn, meat, fish, and wild plants

The Chitamacha lived along the warm waters of the Gulf Coast and inland along freshwater lakes and rivers that flowed into the sea. The mild climate of the area, combined with fertile river-valley soils, enabled them to raise large corn crops. They built square, peaked-roof houses along the water's edge that stood high off the damp, spongy ground. They framed them with wooden poles and covered them with palmetto thatch.

The Chitamacha planted corn, beans, and pumpkin. Corn supplied them with most of their food. They also gathered and preserved quantities of edible wild morning glory and water lily seeds. Men hunted deer and a variety of small animals, fished for catfish, and caught turtles, alligators, and crabs.

Men wore breechcloths and women short skirts woven from grass or other plant fibers.

The Chitamacha believe in the Great Spirit and hold a week-long festival each summer to initiate boys into adulthood.

The French declared war on the Chitamacha in 1706 and within twelve years many of the Indians were dead. Surviving Chitamacha were forced into slavery or relocated on land the French called reservations. Some of the Chitamacha escaped and married Acadians, who had moved south from Canada.

Descendants of the Chitamacha operate a new tribal center on their reservation in southern Louisiana. The women of the tribe continue in the tradition of their ancestors, who were expert weavers, creating finely woven, split-cane mats and baskets, which they sell.

CHOCTAW

(CHAHK-taw)

MEANING OF NAME: Unknown

CULTURE AREA: Southeast

LOCATION: Central and southern Mississippi, and southwestern Alabama

DWELLING TYPE: Thatched houses

CLOTHING MATERIAL: Skins

TRANSPORTATION: Pine and cedar dugout canoes

FOOD: Corn, meat, fish, and wild plants

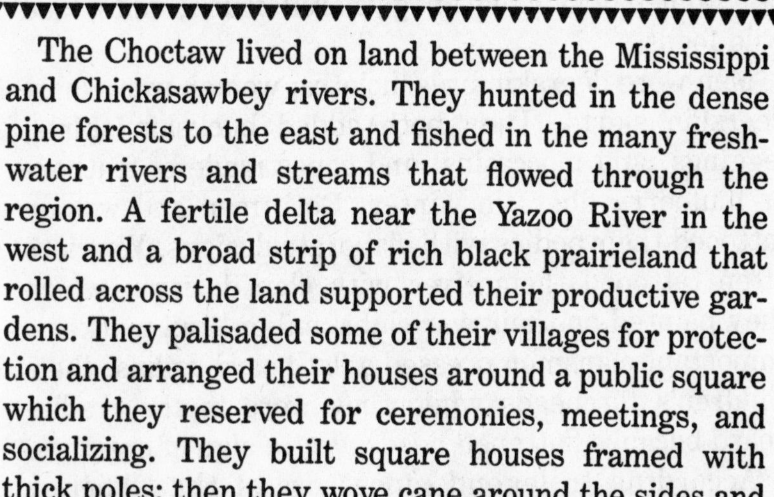

The Choctaw lived on land between the Mississippi and Chickasawbey rivers. They hunted in the dense pine forests to the east and fished in the many freshwater rivers and streams that flowed through the region. A fertile delta near the Yazoo River in the west and a broad strip of rich black prairieland that rolled across the land supported their productive gardens. They palisaded some of their villages for protection and arranged their houses around a public square which they reserved for ceremonies, meetings, and socializing. They built square houses framed with thick poles; then they wove cane around the sides and covered them completely with clay and grass.

Corn, beans, and squash supplied the Choctaw with most of their food. Warm year-round temperatures and abundant rainfall allowed them to produce a sur-

CHOCTAW NATION CAPITOL, c. 1900

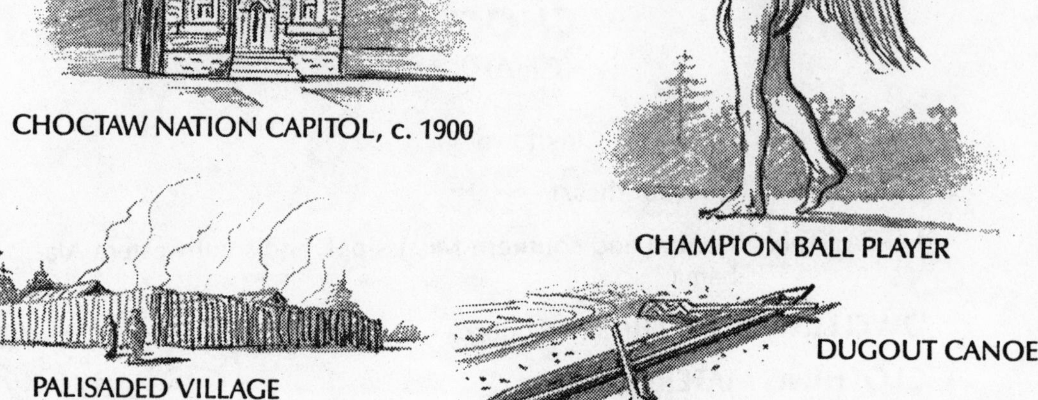

CHAMPION BALL PLAYER

PALISADED VILLAGE

DUGOUT CANOE

plus of corn each year, which they used for trading with trappers and with other tribes. In the spring and fall women and children gathered fruits, nuts, and wild foods.

Men wore deerskin breechcloths; women wore short deerskin skirts. They both added buckskin shirts, leggings, and moccasins, and capes made of feathers or mulberry fibers in winter. Both men and women tattooed their bodies with elaborate designs. Warriors often tattooed themselves with clan designs, which they painted on their war clubs and on trail markers. Important clansmen pressed a flat board against their children's foreheads when they were in the cradle-board because flattened heads were a sign of prestige.

According to legend, ancestors of the Choctaw emerged from beneath a huge mound called "Nanih Waya." In a celebration called the Green Corn Festival, the Choctaw give thanks each year for their bountiful harvest.

The Choctaw fought under General Andrew Jackson

in the War of 1812, but Jackson failed to help them when Spain gave their land to white settlers. As president of the United States, he introduced into Congress in 1830 the Indian Removal Act, which called for the removal of all eastern Indians to Indian Territory west of the Mississippi River. Many Choctaw died on the forced march westward, but within thirty years, their survivors had produced surplus crops from the new land. As a member of the Five Civilized Tribes, the Choctaw adopted a democratic form of government with a constitution, courts, and regular elections—a government that was forcibly dissolved in 1907, when Oklahoma achieved statehood. The Choctaw also lost most of their reservation land to white settlers.

Descendants of the Choctaw live in Oklahoma and Mississippi.

CHUMASH

(CHOO-mahsh)

MEANING OF NAME: Unknown

CULTURE AREA: California

LOCATION: Southern California and the Channel Islands

DWELLING TYPE: Grass-covered houses

CLOTHING MATERIAL: Skins

TRANSPORTATION: Wooden plank canoes

FOOD: Acorns, fish, meat, and wild plants

The Chumash made their home along the Pacific Coast from San Luis Obispo to Malibu Canyon and inland to the San Joaquin Valley, as well as on the Channel Islands. It is an area of long mountain ranges, broad valleys, freshwater rivers, and dry plains. Food resources were limitless and the Indians lived entirely off the land all year. On the hilly rugged offshore islands, strong winds and constant mild temperatures provided excellent fishing. The Chumash built their villages on high ground where streams ran into the sea. Several family homes, a ceremonial enclosure, a gambling area, and a cemetery filled each village. They constructed their houses in the shape of large hemispheres, which they framed with poles and covered with a thick layer of grass. About seventy people lived in each house.

Acorns provided most of the food. The Chumash also gathered pine nuts, berries, seeds, roots, and quantities of fish. Men snared rabbits and shot geese and ducks, which migrated north each year. Along the coast and on the islands, fish and shellfish were abundant. Seals, sea otters, porpoises, and pilot whales were also available to the hunters.

The men built long wood-plank canoes by "sewing" the planks together with plant and animal fibers. They used pitch for caulking and painted or decorated the canoes with shells. They paddled their boats along the Santa Barbara Channel Islands all the way to San Nicolas Island, sixty-five miles from the mainland.

Men wore only a string or a piece of fiber netting around their waists, and to it they attached small objects, tools, or hunting implements. Women wore knee-length buckskin fringed aprons decorated with snail and abalone shells. When it was cold, everyone wore shirts and waist-length fur robes made of bird

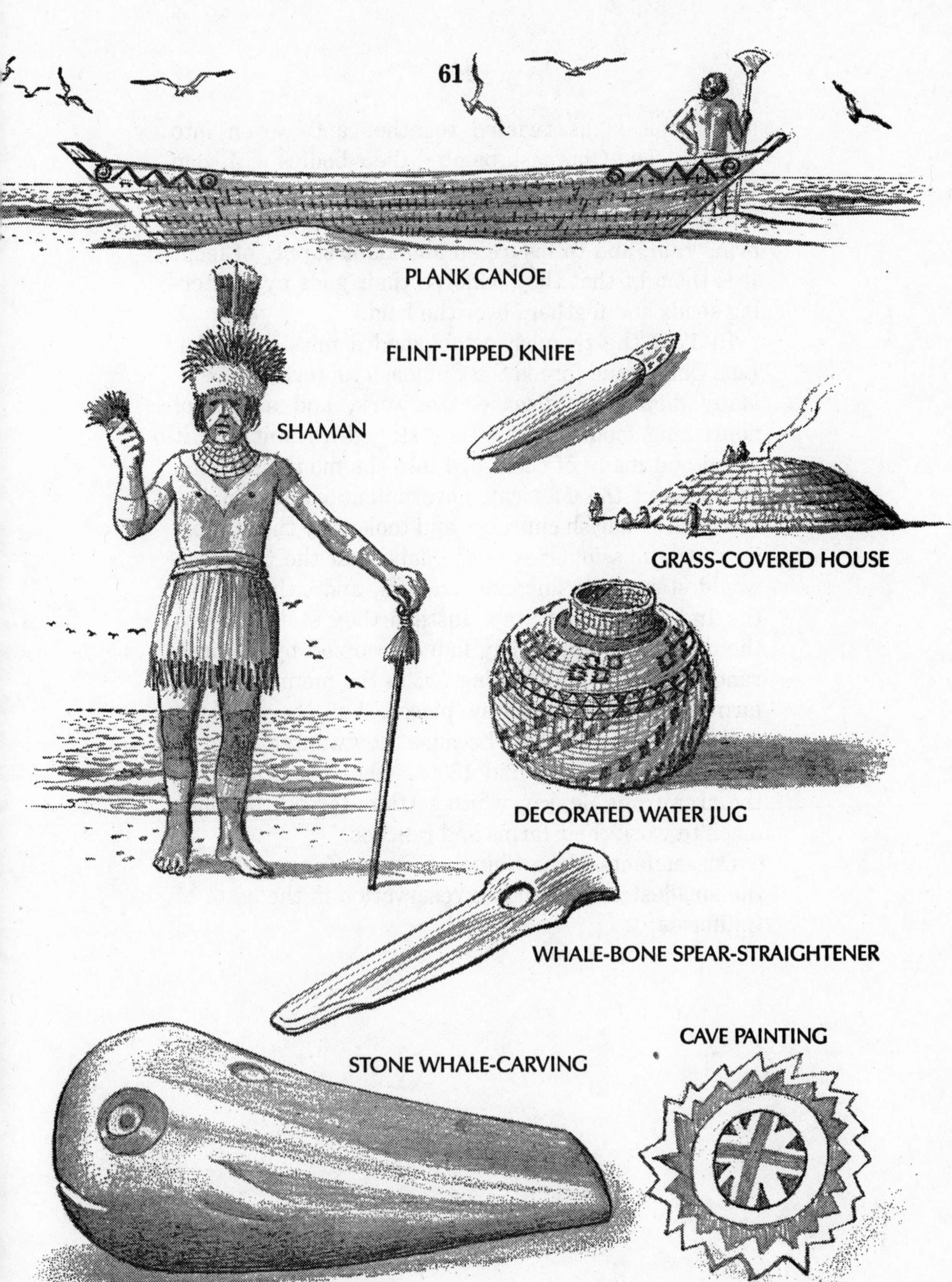
PLANK CANOE
FLINT-TIPPED KNIFE
SHAMAN
GRASS-COVERED HOUSE
DECORATED WATER JUG
WHALE-BONE SPEAR-STRAIGHTENER
CAVE PAINTING
STONE WHALE-CARVING

and rabbit skins twisted together and woven into squares. The Chumash painted their bodies with clan designs for easy identification.

The Chumash employed shamans to cure illness, to bring rain, and to insure an abundant supply of food. It is thought that they honored their gods by scattering seeds and feathers over the land.

In 1772 the Spanish established a mission at San Luis Obispo and forced the Chumash to work for them. Many died from disease, overwork, and a lack of nourishing food. In 1824 they staged a revolt, but it failed and many of them fled into the mountains. Ten years later the Mexican government converted the missions to parish churches and took away the authority of the missionaries in the hope that the Chumash would stay on as farmers, traders, and citizens. But the Indians did not stay. Instead they stole away to their villages, which they found occupied by Mexican ranchers. They tried hiding out in the mountains and farming in out-of-the-way places, but the Mexican ranchers harassed them because they wanted them as ranch hands. In the mid 1800s, when America took the area from Mexico, white settlers forced the Chumash to work their farms and ranches.

Descendants of the Chumash live on Zange de Cota, the smallest official Indian reservation in the state of California.

COMANCHE

(ke-MAN-chee)

MEANING OF NAME: Those who are always against us

CULTURE AREA: Plains

LOCATION: Northern Texas, eastern Oklahoma, southwestern Kansas, and southwestern Colorado

DWELLING TYPE: Tipis

CLOTHING MATERIAL: Skins

TRANSPORTATION: Horses

FOOD: Meat and wild plants

The Comanche lived in high country, five thousand feet above sea level, in a rugged mountainous region that now includes four separate states. During the winter hunting season they lived in skin-covered tipis, which they placed in rows in sheltered canyons. There they hunted deer, elk, antelope, and smaller animals. In spring, when the buffalo came, they moved onto the plains and arranged their tipis in well-organized circles. Many tipis had stripes and geometric designs painted on their skin coverings. Buffalo hunting was a communal activity requiring the cooperation of many hunters. Each hunt was preceded by sacred ceremonies. When it was very warm, some families preferred to live in small brush-covered shelters instead of in their tipis.

Buffalo meat supplied the Comanche with most of

their food, and they used the remainder of the animal to make clothes, tipi covers, tools, and utensils. Brave, skillful hunters used fourteen-foot lances instead of bows and arrows to kill buffalo, because hunting with a lance was a mark of pride. They skewered meat on pointed sticks and cooked it over hot coals or cut it into strips to dry in the sun. They made a mushy mixture of buffalo marrow and mesquite beans, which was very popular. They made pemmican, too, adding nuts, marrow, and fat to dried meat. It was easy to trade their pemmican for tasty pumpkin seeds, honey, and tobacco. Wherever the Comanche made camp, the women collected fruits and berries, nuts and wild greens.

Men wore buckskin breechcloths and shirts, and moccasins with tough buffalo-skin soles. Sometimes they decorated their moccasins with beads and paint and greased them to make them waterproof. Women wore buckskin shirts and long, finely decorated fringed skirts. When it was cold they all wore leggings and buffalo-skin robes with the fur on the inside. Comanche men claimed they could identify anyone's footprint in the snow or mud by observing the sole, heel fringe, and toe design of the moccasin.

To the Comanche, as to most other Indian tribes, religion is a very private matter. They believe in supernatural forces and that the power to deal with nature's mysteries can be achieved by having a vision.

The Comanche rode into Mexico and joined tribes of the Kiowa as soon as they acquired horses. They raided bands of Apache and other Indian enemies and lost many warriors. They replaced their losses by capturing both Indian and White women and children. They signed an agreement allowing emigrants safe passage through their lands if the Texas troopers

BRUSH SHELTER, TIPI, MEAT-DRYING RACK
PAINTED-SKIN SHIELD
WAR WHISTLE
SKIN CLOTHING
PAINTED-HIDE CARRYING CASE
BEADED SKIN POUCH
POWDER HORN
COLLAR FOR PET ANTELOPE WITH METAL JINGLERS

would help to confine the intruders to one trail so they would not scare away the buffalo. The troopers could not control the settlers, and the Comanche eventually ceded their lands and moved to reservations. When Texas was still a republic, its citizens organized the Texas Rangers to drive Indians out of the territory, including the tribes living on reservation lands. Many of the Comanche escaped the Rangers and joined neighboring bands, particularly the Kiowa, who were experts at raiding white settlements. In 1868, however, the Comanche agreed to move to a reservation in Indian Territory. The United States Government broke its promise to supply food to the Indians living on the reservation, and many of them starved to death. Later their reservation land was divided among tribal members who received parcels of land and white settlers who bought the remaining land.

Descendants of the Comanche live in Oklahoma, where they are successful farmers and cattlemen.

CREEK
(KREEK)

MEANING OF NAME: The many creeks upon which they lived

CULTURE AREA: Southeast

LOCATION: Alabama, Georgia, and Tennessee

DWELLING TYPE: Thatched houses

CLOTHING MATERIAL: Skins

TRANSPORTATION: Wooden dugout canoes

FOOD: Corn, meat, fish, and wild plants

The Creek lived in a rolling valley between the Appalachian Mountains and the coastal plains of the Atlantic Ocean. The Upper Creek lived along the Coosa, Tallapoosa, and Alabama rivers, and the Lower Creek lived along the waters of the Chattahoochee River. They hunted and fished throughout their territory, exploiting every natural resource it provided. They framed their houses with poles, wove cane around the sides, and covered them with clay and grass. Clan members clustered their dwellings close together so they could share meals. In the center of their village they built a large dome-shaped, earth-covered Council House, where they conducted religious ceremonies. Some of the wealthy families often owned a second house and used it to store their belongings.

The Creek cultivated three types of corn as well as beans, squash, pumpkin, and tobacco. Corn supplied them with most of their food. Whole families went on extended hunting trips in search of game, particularly deer, bear, and turkey. They collected and preserved wild potatoes and a variety of berries.

The men wore deerskin breechcloths and the women wore short deerskin skirts. They added moccasins and fur robes when it was cold.

The Creek worship the Sun and believe that the Great Spirit gives them the black drink, which is reserved for important celebrations. Each year they express their thanks for a bountiful harvest by danc-

ing, feasting and praying at the Green Corn Festival.

In 1812 General Andrew Jackson and Cherokee troops defeated the Creek at the Battle of Horseshoe Bend, which was fought in the great loop of the Tallapoosa River at Tohopeka, Alabama. After their defeat, the Creek were forced to cede twenty-three million acres of their land, one-half of the state of Alabama. Twenty years later they lost the rest of their land when President Jackson ignored a treaty of ownership signed by his predecessor, President John Quincy Adams. Weakened by betrayal, fraudulent deals, and illegal treaties, the Creek agreed to move to Indian Territory in 1836. Fourteen thousand Creek were packed into steamboats and sent down the Alabama River, across the Gulf of Mexico to New Orleans, and up the Mississippi River to Rock Roe, in Arkansas Territory. They walked more than three hundred miles to reservation land in Indian Territory. Thirty-five hundred of their number died along the way from dysentery, cholera, and from drowning when an overloaded steamboat sank. Survivors built towns, raised crops, reestablished their tribal government, and set up European-style schools on their reservation. As one of the Five Civilized Tribes, they developed a democratic form of government and adopted a constitution, a court system, and regular elections. In the early 1900s, however, their government, which had served its people for almost three-quarters of a century, was dissolved by edict of the United States government and their reservation was reduced in size. Tribal members received parcels of land and the United States Government sold the rest to white settlers. Not all of the Creek moved to Oklahoma as directed, however. Some fled to Florida and joined the Seminole.

Descendants of the Creek people live in Florida, Alabama, and Oklahoma.

CROW

(KRO)

MEANING OF NAME: Children of the large-beaked bird (a corrupted French translation)

CULTURE AREA: Plains

LOCATION: Southwestern Montana and northern Wyoming

DWELLING TYPE: Tipis

CLOTHING MATERIAL: Skins

TRANSPORTATION: Skin bullboats, horses, and snowshoes

FOOD: Meat and wild plants

The Crow lived along the Yellowstone River, one of the largest tributaries of the Missouri River. They hunted bear, elk, and deer in the Rocky Mountains from Glacier National Park in northern Montana to Yellowstone National Park in the southern part of the state. Hunters wore deerskin disguises and crept around on their hands and knees to surprise browsing deer. In the spring, however, large herds of buffalo came to feed on the tall grass of the eastern plains and bands of the Crow followed them. The Indians set up their large skin-covered tipis in circles and carefully organized their hunters, who skillfully chased the herds from horseback and drove them over cliffs.

Buffalo meat supplied the Crow with most of their food, clothing, tipi coverings, and household utensils. Women and children collected berries, roots, and other wild foods wherever they made camp. Some of the men cultivated small crops of tobacco to smoke during religious ceremonies.

The men wore buckskin aprons and leggings and, for special occasions, finely tanned leather shirts. The women wore long sheepskin or deerskin dresses and knee-high leggings. They decorated their formal dresses with elk teeth or dyed porcupine quills. Robes and moccasins of buffalo hides with the fur turned inside kept them warm in cold weather.

The Crow believe that the god, Itsihbadhis, possesses all the elements that existed before the world began, and that Old Man, their mythological hero, is a trickster and a teacher.

The Crow traded with the Shoshone for horses. Many died during a smallpox epidemic in 1822 and the survivors allied themselves with the Americans, fighting against tribes of the Sioux and Nez Perce. They

TIPI, BOTTOM ROLLED UP FOR SUMMER COMFORT

WOMEN'S SHELL EARRINGS

MEN'S HAIR ORNAMENTS

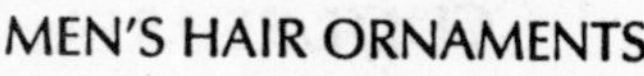

BULLBOAT

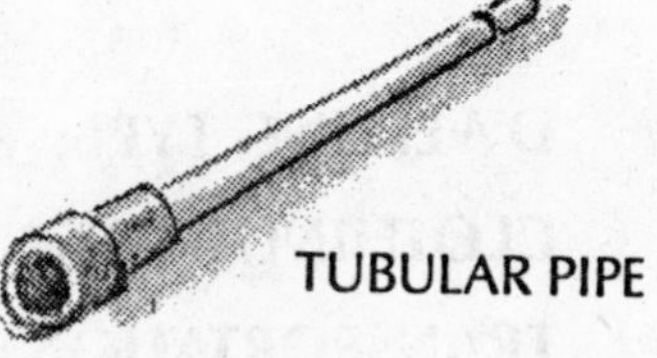

TUBULAR PIPE

hoped that the alliance would enable them to stay in their homeland, but in 1851 they were forced to move to a reservation in Montana. Most of the reservation land was taken back fifteen years later, but the Crow did not really care because the buffalo herds had disappeared from the plains, taking with them the culture of their people.

Today descendants of the Crow farm, ranch, and entertain tourists on their high plains reservation in southeastern Montana, under which Mother Earth holds seventeen billion tons of coal.

DELAWARE

(DEL-eh-wer)

MEANING OF NAME: Unknown

CULTURE AREA: Northeast

LOCATION: New Jersey, Delaware, New York, and eastern Pennsylvania

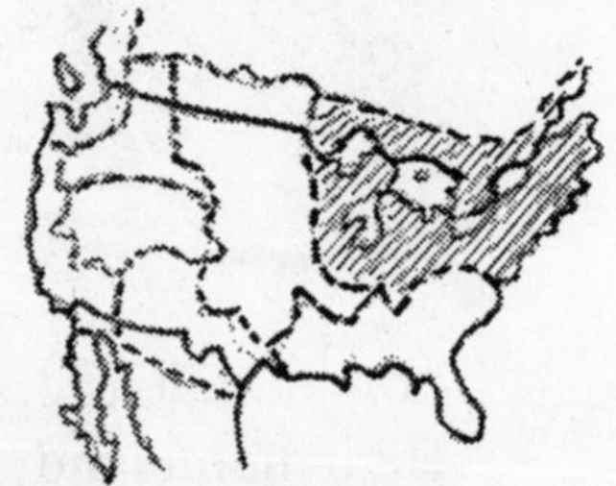

DWELLING TYPE: Barrel-shaped longhouses

CLOTHING MATERIAL: Skins

TRANSPORTATION: Pine dugout canoes

FOOD: Corn, meat, fish, and wild plants

The Delaware, who called themselves Lenni Lenapi, lived in northern New Jersey, southern New York, and southeastern Pennsylvania in a region filled with freshwater rivers, a lush, varied coastline, and the forests of the Catskill Mountains. Several large rivers feed the region—the Delaware, Schuylkill, and Hudson—producing fertile waters and rich riverbanks. The Delaware built pitched-roofed, barrel-shaped dwellings, which they framed with arched saplings and covered with bark. Several related families lived in each house.

The Delaware were primarily farmers, who planted large gardens of corn, beans, pumpkin, squash, and tobacco. They planted in the spring and spent the summer along rivers and streams near the coast digging for shellfish and building freshwater stone weirs

CEREMONIAL HOUSE

AUTUMN CLOTHING

HUNTER'S SPIRIT MASK

FINE DUGOUT CANOE

for trapping fish. They returned home in the fall to harvest their crops. The women collected nuts, berries, roots, and maple sap, and the men hunted for beaver, muskrat, and white-tailed deer. They snared the deer or drove them into enclosures.

The men wore belted deerskin aprons and moccasins, and the women wore knee-length deerskin skirts. They both wore leather shirts, leggings, and moccasins, decorating them with shells, beads, and porcupine quills. When it was cold they wore woven turkey-feather robes or fur robes tied over one shoulder with a separate sleeve to cover the otherwise bare arm.

The Delaware believe Great Manitou and his subordinate spirits are present in all living things. They have recorded their history with bark paintings and wood carvings that tell tribal stories.

The Dutch massacred hundreds of the Delaware during the 1600s in an effort to take away their land and dominate the fur trade. Even though William Penn guaranteed the Delaware their land in a 1686 treaty, the treaty was ignored and most of their land was taken by white settlers. Between 1778 and 1830, the Delawares signed several dozen treaties in an effort to remain in their homeland, but the treaties were ignored. Many Delaware moved to Canada, Ohio, and Missouri because they were not given reservation land of their own and were at the mercy of other Indian tribes to give them a place to live. The Missouri group prospered as farmers, but that land too was taken away and they were forced to move to Kansas to start over again. Then in 1866, the Kansas land was also taken from them and they were sent to Indian Territory to live with the Wichita and Caddo on their reservation.

Many descendants of the widely scattered Delaware live in Oklahoma, Wisconsin, Pennsylvania, and Ontario, Canada.

GABRIELINO
(gahbreel-EENO)

MEANING OF NAME: Taken from the name of the San Gabriel mission

CULTURE AREA: California

LOCATION: California and the islands of San Clemente, Santa Catalina, and San Nicolas

DWELLING TYPE: Mat-covered round houses

CLOTHING MATERIALS: Skins and fibers

TRANSPORTATION: Skin bullboats

FOOD: Fish, meat, and wild plants

The Gabrielino lived in southern California along the coast in what is now Los Angeles and Orange County, and on the offshore islands. They established permanent villages along the coastline and built dome-shaped, round houses, which they framed with saplings and covered with mats made of tule leaves, ferns, and other plants. Each village had a large, round, earth-covered sweat lodge dug below ground that was used by the men for bathing and socializing. They held important ceremonies in an oval-shaped roofless enclosure, which they built near the chief's home. It was made by pushing willow poles into the ground and weaving smaller branches around the sides.

The rich resources of the area enabled the Gabrielino to live entirely off the land. Men hunted deer, sea

mammals, and small animals. They dug shellfish, fished along the coast, and fished for salmon and other large fish on inland rivers and streams. Each fall, families collected acorns, pine nuts, and a variety of wild plants.

Gabrielino men did not wear clothes, but they wore woven yucca sandals when they went hunting in the mountains. Women wore two-sided aprons of deerskin or woven bark, and when it was cold everyone wore capes of deerskin, rabbit fur, or birdskin and feathers.

The Gabrielino believe that the crow, raven, owl, and eagle are sacred creatures, and they use eagle feathers when performing religious rituals because a dying chief once told them he would return in the form of an eagle.

The Spanish called the Gabrielino "White Indians" because their skin was very light. When the Spanish established the San Gabriel Mission in 1771, they forced the Gabrielino to join the mission. Many of them died from disease, overwork, and lack of nourishing food. They are now believed to be an extinct native group.

HAIDA
(HY-deh)

MEANING OF NAME: People

CULTURE AREA: Northwest

LOCATION: British Columbia and Alaska

DWELLING TYPE: Plank houses

CLOTHING MATERIALS: Bark and skins

TRANSPORTATION: Cedar dugout canoes

FOOD: Fish, meat, and wild plants

The Haida lived on the Queen Charlotte and Prince of Wales islands, which are submerged peaks belonging to the Coast Range. The islands are surrounded by steep-sided rocky bluffs and are covered with dense cedar forests. The Queen Charlotte Islands once produced the tallest cedars along the northwest coast as well as some of the region's best woodworkers. The forests supplied the Haida with most of their building materials for houses, clothes, and household utensils. Unlike the hardwood trees of the northeast, cedar trees can be split into straight, even planks, or boards. They can also be carved, cut evenly, and shaped, using only stone axes and mauls. The Haida built large

"HAWK" PAINTED FACE

COASTAL VILLAGE

WHALING IN DUGOUT CANOE

permanent villages set back from the coastline, their rectangular-shaped houses facing the ocean. The houses were framed with large timbers and covered with long cedar planks. Ten or twelve families, belonging to either the Raven or Eagle clans, shared one large house. Many of the houses had a single carved pole displaying clan figures in front of the house where the roof was gabled. Others had carved posts at each end of the house and a painted front.

Haida men fished for salmon, halibut, and other fish, which supplied them with most of their food. They hunted seals, sea lions, and sea otters along the rocky coast, but found few land animals on the islands except black bears, which came to feed on the islands' rich crops of berries and fish. The Haida were known to capture members of neighboring tribes, particularly Indians with little status or wealth.

The men wore no clothes; the women wore woven cedar-bark skirts. They both used double-woven cedar-bark capes and blankets or heavy fur when it was cold. They tattooed their bodies with family crests, and children from wealthy families had special tattoos on their chests and on the backs of their hands to make them easy to identify.

Some of the Haida men became master woodworkers who crafted houses, canoes, boxes, and other utensils from wood. They built fifty-foot ocean-going dugout canoes from huge cedar logs. They painted and carved the prows and sterns in the shape of birds and animals, displaying their artistic skills. They traded their crafts and boats with the Tsimshian Indians for candlefish oil and Chilkat blankets, which were made of interwoven cedar bark and mountain goat wool. Throughout the northwest, expertly crafted Haida canoes were desired by other tribes who traded for them whenever possible.

The Haida believe in supernatural ocean beings, which disguise themselves as fish and sea mammals. They borrowed many ceremonies and myths from the Tlingit and Tsimshain, changing the stories to suit their needs. Clans and groups of the Haida displayed their wealth and importance by hosting extravagant "potlatch" parties during the winter.

European explorers and traders visited the Haida, and the Hudson Bay Company opened a post in their territory in 1869. Later many Haida died from European diseases. By the mid 1900s their population was one-tenth its original size due to the introduction of alcohol and foreign disease. Later, their land was taken over by commercial canning and lumbering operations.

Descendants of the Haida live on the Queen Charlotte Islands.

HAVASUPI

(hah-veh-SOO-py)

MEANING OF NAME: The people who lived at the place that is green

CULTURE AREA: Southwest

LOCATION: Arizona

DWELLING TYPE: Brush lean-tos

CLOTHING MATERIALS: Skins and fiber

TRANSPORTATION: Unknown

FOOD: Meat, wild plants, and corn

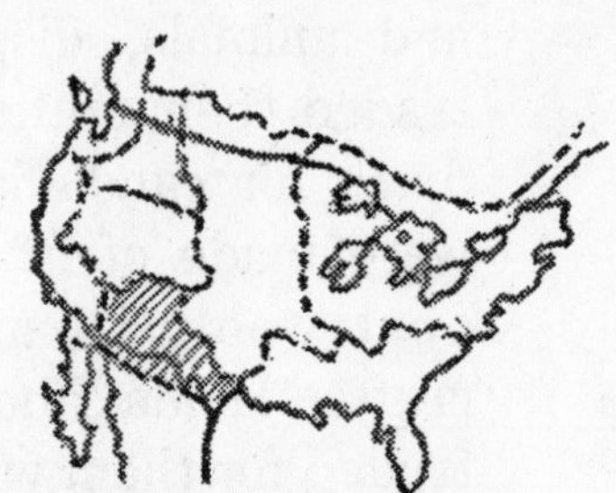

The Havasupi lived on a small green patch of land three hundred feet below the rim of a canyon that forms a branch of the Grand Canyon. They built simple brush lean-tos, which they framed with two upright forked poles and a crossbeam covered with poles, twigs, and brush.

The Havasupi traveled along special routes each season in search of food. They also planted very small gardens of corn, beans, squash, and sunflowers, using seeds given to them by their neighbors, the Hopi, who had taught them how to farm. They built earth or brush dams around their garden plots to trap and direct rainwater. Wearing animal disguises, men hunted small animals and stalked antelope, deer, and bighorn sheep. In winter the Havasupi lived on the canyon rim and stored surplus foods below them in caves in the canyon walls. Some families spent the

winter months with their neighbors, the Hopi and Walapais, in northern Arizona.

Havasupi men wore bark or hide breechcloths and sandals of woven juniper bark; the women wore two-sided bark aprons and leg wrappings. They both wore fur blankets, robes, moccasins, and muffs in the winter. By the 1800s they had adopted leather clothing similar to that worn by their Plains neighbors.

A boy and his grandmother are two mythological figures who are important to the Havasupi. Little information is revealed about the grandmother, but the boy lives in the east and travels west each year to visit his grandmother, bringing with him rain, wind, and seeds to scatter upon the earth.

Missionaries, trappers, Hopi, and Navajo came into the canyon in the late 1700s, scaring away the game and trampling their forage. When lead was discovered in the canyon, miners trampled the gardens of the Indians and threatened their precious crops. In the late 1800s, a tiny piece of the Havasupi homeland was made into a reservation.

Descendants still live in the canyon, where they raise money by operating tourist accommodations.

HOPI

(HO-pee)

MEANING OF NAME: Peaceful ones

CULTURE AREA: Southwest

LOCATION: Northern Arizona

DWELLING TYPE: Multifamily adobe houses

CLOTHING MATERIALS: Skins and cotton

TRANSPORTATION: Unknown

FOOD: Corn, wild plants, and meat

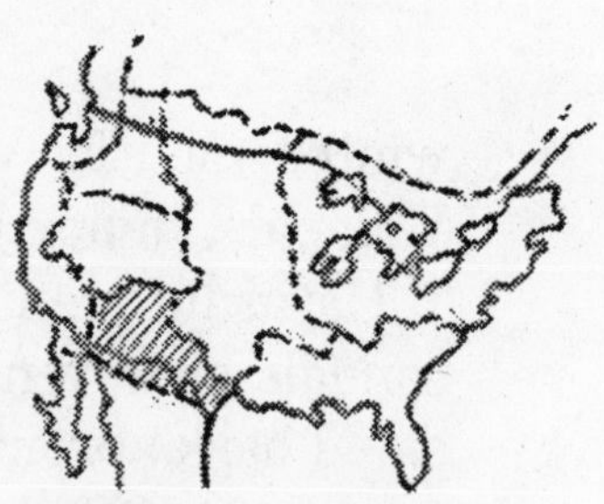

The Hopi live in northern Arizona on top of three mesas that were cut from Black Mesa long ago by streams of the Tusayan washes. Besides carving the mesas, the washes deposited sand and silt on the plains below. The Hopi have lived in one mesa top village, Oraibi, for more than a thousand years. At one time all their other villages were situated in the valley, but the Hopi moved to the mesa tops to protect themselves from Spanish invasions. They built their adobe houses three stories high—never higher—and connected them in long rows. The roof of each house serves as a terrace for the house above and ladders make it easy to climb from house to house.

Corn has been the basis of Hopi life for thousands of

years despite the harsh, dry environment. Often subjected to long periods of drought, their crops seldom fail. The Hopi have been able to coax corn, beans, and squash to grow in the sandy desert soil for many generations because Black Mesa soil remains trapped in the valley and there are several permanent springs nearby to help native gardeners. Garden plots are owned by individual clans, who mark them off at the corners with rocks painted with clan symbols. Hopi men tend the gardens and plant several varieties of corn, many kinds of beans, squash, and pumpkins. They also grow gourds and make them into dippers, cups, rattles, scrapers, and containers. Women gathered many berries, nuts, and seeds in the desert. Men organized rabbit hunts using throwing sticks, even though hunting was never an important activity for them.

The men wore wide, flapping, cotton pants and loose shirts and moccasins; women wore knee-length hand-woven belted dresses that crossed over the right shoulder, leaving the left one free. They wore moccasins and wrapped their legs in buckskin from the knees to the ankles to protect them from prickly desert plants when collecting wild foods.

The Hopi celebrate the winter solstice each year, repeating legends of their migration and watching masked dancers, called katchinas, imitate the rain gods. Their children believe the masked dancers are really rain gods who have come to visit their village. To learn about the many different rain gods, children are given small carved and painted dolls made in imitation of the masked katchinas to take home—for study but not for play.

The Spanish established missions among the Hopi and tried unsuccessfully to take away their native religion. When the Hopi joined the Pueblo Revolt in 1680, they drove the Spanish away forever. It was during and after this revolt that they moved their villages onto the mesa tops. After the revolt the Hopis eliminated their one Christianized village and have continued ever since to resist missionary appeals. Although their villages are on the top of the mesas, they also own the land in the valley below. For many years the Navajo settled on this land and the Hopi ignored their presence. Today these land rights are at issue.

The Hopi still live in their mesa-top villages in northeastern Arizona.

KAROK

(KA-rahk)

MEANING OF NAME: Upstream

CULTURE AREA: California

LOCATION: Northern California

DWELLING TYPE: Plank-covered lodges

CLOTHING MATERIALS: Skins and bark

TRANSPORTATION: Snowshoes

FOOD: Fish, acorns, meat, and wild plants

The Karok lived close to the Pacific coastline along the middle course of the Klamath River and its tributaries, which flow south from the California-Oregon State borders. They hunted in the Trinity Mountains and gathered a large annual crop of acorns in the foothills. They built permanent villages with a sweat house standing in the center. It was reserved for men for bathing, socializing, and sleeping. The Karok dug foundations for their houses four or five feet below ground, framed the shell with logs, and covered it with thick wooden planks. The women and children lived in the houses, but the men spent all their time in the sweat house, coming home only for meals. Women were allowed into the sweat house only for the initiation of a female shaman.

The Karok followed an annual cycle of fishing, hunting, and wild-food gathering, which provided them

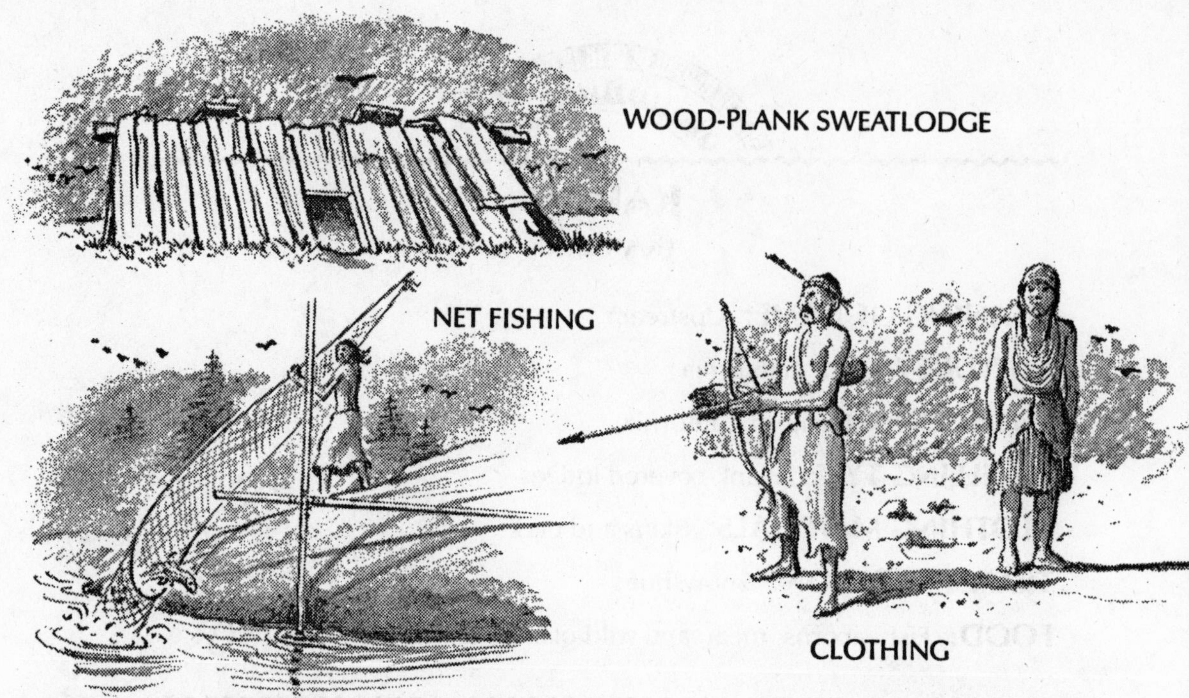

with food all year round. They celebrated the salmon's swim upriver in spring by netting or spearing hundreds of spawning fish, many of which they smoked. They lived in bark shelters during the fall, when they camped in their favorite acorn groves. The men drove elk and deer into snares using specially trained dogs. They smoked rodents out of their holes and dragged bears out of their dens. They also collected a variety of birds, lizards, frogs, grasshoppers, and caterpillars.

Many of the Karok men wore no clothes. Some wore buckskin breechcloths. Women wore two-sided, fringed leather aprons and deerskin capes. When hunting in the mountains, the men wore leggings and moccasins with thick elk-hide soles. Basketlike hats covered their heads. They decorated their formal clothing with shells, nuts, and fancy grasses or wove them of maple bark.

The Karok believe in the Morning and Evening Stars

and that the Milky Way is the road to the dead. They celebrate the Jumping Dance and Deerskin Dance each year to allow their leaders a chance to display their wealth. Wealth and status, which were important to the Karok, were also put on display each winter at extravagant potlatch parties.

In the late 1800s, the Karok initiated the Ghost Dance ceremonies in an effort to rid the world of white people through supernatural means. They believed that the dances would also bring back Indians who knew what the world was like before the whites had come. They also thought the ceremonies would restore their land and resources.

The Karok traded with trappers in the 1700s. By 1850 gold miners had invaded their territory and burned most of their villages. When the Karok sought the help of government soldiers, many of the Indians were murdered. Over a hundred Karok were killed before the mines gave out and the miners left in the late 1800s.

Descendants of the Karok live on a reservation and in communities along the Klamath River in California.

KICKAPOO

(KICK-eh-poo)

MEANING OF NAME: Unknown

CULTURE AREA: Northeast

LOCATION: Illinois and Wisconsin

DWELLING TYPES: Longhouses and brush shelters

CLOTHING MATERIAL: Skins

TRANSPORTATION: Horses

FOOD: Meat, corn, and wild plants

The Kickapoo moved too often to be associated with a specific area, but they lived mostly in southern Wisconsin and central Illinois in the late 1700s. When the government later forced them to move to Indian Territory, the tribe became permanently divided: one group settled in Indian Territory that later became central Oklahoma, and the other group settled in northern Mexico. The Oklahoma group built semipermanent villages with rectangular, bark-covered houses framed with poles. In the summer many built smaller dome-shaped houses covered with mats. The Mexican group lived in temporary brush shelters to accommodate their new nomadic lifestyle.

The Oklahoma Kickapoo planted gardens of corn, beans, and squash near their villages and the women collected fruits, nuts, and greens all year. Small family groups often hunted deer and bear together in the mountains or went on longer trips westward in search of buffalo. The southern group became expert raiders and scavengers.

Men wore buckskin breechcloths; women wore short leather skirts. They both wore fur capes, leggings, and moccasins when it was cold.

The Kickapoo believe in Great Manitou, the Creator, and they tell stories at small private feasts during the winter when the spirits are believed to be sleeping.

For many years the Kickapoo fought against the French, and other Indian tribes. They allied themselves with tribes of the Sauk and Fox Indians and

defeated the Illinois Indians, whose land they kept. After the War of 1812, American veterans were awarded parcels of land that belonged to the Indians living in Illinois. Although the Indians fought to keep settlers off their land, the Kickapoo were forced to cede it and move to Missouri. White squatters forced the Kickapoo off the Missouri land and the Indians moved once again, this time to Kansas. When the railroad came to Kansas, however, the Kickapoo were forced to move yet again to a reservation in Indian Territory in Oklahoma. (This was when one group went to Mexico. They became known as the Mexican Kickapoo.) The Oklahoma reservation was later divided among tribal members and white settlers who wanted to buy land. The Kickapoo refused to divide their holdings and negotiated for many years to hold the land in common. Eventually they were fooled into signing an illegal agreement that divided it.

Descendants of the Kickapoo live in Kansas, Oklahoma, and Mexico.

KIOWA

(KY-o-wa)

MEANING OF NAME: A people who paint the two halves of the body or face different colors

CULTURE AREA: Plains

LOCATION: Southwestern Oklahoma and Texas

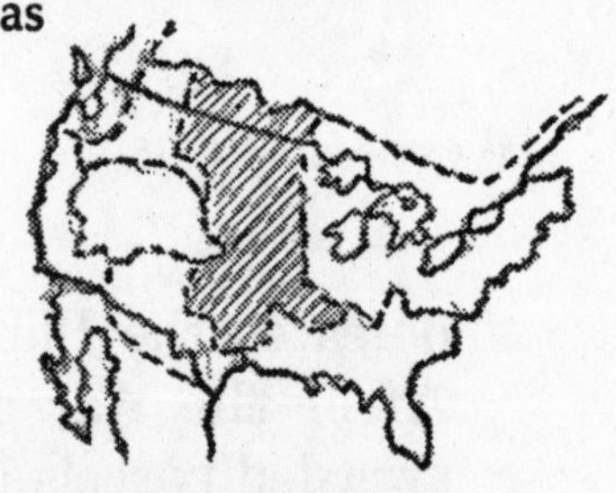

DWELLING TYPE: Tipis

CLOTHING MATERIAL: Skins

TRANSPORTATION: Horses

FOOD: Meat and wild plants

The Kiowa lived near the Wichita Mountains, where the broad waters of the Red River form a boundary between Oklahoma and Texas. An area rich with wildlife and abundant water sources, it was also surrounded by grassy plains. The Kiowa lived in sheltered valleys during the winter, where small bands set up skin-covered tipis to hunt deer and antelope. In the summer, when buffalo herds roamed the plains, all the groups moved from the valleys and set up beautifully colored tipis in large circles. The painted skins of the tipis told the history of the tribe. Buffalo hunting was a communal activity that began with sacred ceremonies and required the cooperation of many hunters.

The Kiowa drove the buffalo herds over cliffs or surrounded them and drove them into enclosures. Buffalo meat supplied most of their food. They made

TIPI FORMAL CLOTHING

pemmican with it and traded it for corn. While the men hunted, women and children gathered berries, nuts, and wild foods wherever they made camp. The Kiowa had strong taboos against eating bears, birds, or fish.

Kiowa men wore deerskin breechcloths and the women wore deerskin dresses, both adding deerskin moccasins and buffalo-fur robes in cold weather.

The Kiowa believe the Sun is the chief god and that owls and other nocturnal birds own the souls of the dead.

The Kiowa became skillful raiders after acquiring horses from their neighbors, the Comanche, who had stolen them from other tribes. Texas Rangers, organized by settlers to rid the state of all Indians, killed many Kiowa and then forced the survivors to move to a reservation in Indian Territory. The Kiowa, however, continued to raid settlements from their reservation. A series of measles epidemics eventually killed many of them. When Oklahoma became a state and their reservation was divided, the Kiowa, like so many other Indian tribes, were given parcels of land so that white settlers could buy the remainder of the land.

Descendants of the Kiowa live in Oklahoma.

KLAMATH

(KLAM-ehth)

MEANING OF NAME: Men

CULTURE AREA: California

LOCATION: Southern Oregon and northern California

DWELLING TYPE: Earth lodges

CLOTHING MATERIALS: Fiber and skins

TRANSPORTATION: Wooden dugout canoes

FOOD: Roots, fish, meat, and wild plants

The Klamath lived in the Cascade Mountains of southern Oregon and on the Mococ Plateau in northern California, an area much higher than anywhere else along the coast. Between dense groves of pine, fir, and juniper, pockets of mixed grassland and sagebrush yielded quantities of edible roots. These people built large, round, earth lodges, framing them with logs and covering them with soil and grass. Each village had a communal sweat house, which was reserved for the men for bathing and socializing.

Waterlily roots supplied the Klamath with most of their food, although the varied resources of the area enabled them to fish and hunt and gather wild foods all year. Men netted quantities of fish in freshwater rivers and streams. They hunted deer, antelope, and smaller animals in the mountains. Women and children

EARTH LODGE AND DUGOUT CANOE

BASKET-LIKE HATS

collected a wide variety of nuts, berries, and wild greens.

Klamath men wore breechcloths of buckskin or woven fibers, and the women wore two-sided aprons and basketlike hats. Because it was considered honorable, the Klamath often pressed a flat board against the foreheads of very young babies to flatten them.

The Klamath believe in shamans, who obtain special powers by fasting, praying, and seeking visions from animal spirits, especially birds.

The Klamath and their neighbors, the Modoc, traded horses for slaves along the Columbia River. White settlers in wagon trains destroyed many of their wild foods, scared away their game, and left them sick with strange diseases. Survivors signed a treaty in 1864 ceding most of their land in exchange for a small reservation. Later they sold the reservation land and divided the money among tribal members.

Descendants of the Klamath live in Oregon.

KWAKIUTL

(KWAH-kee-oot-l)

MEANING OF NAME: Beach on the north side of the river

CULTURE AREA: Northwest

LOCATION: Vancouver Island, British Columbia

DWELLING TYPE: Plank houses

CLOTHING MATERIALS: Bark and skin

TRANSPORTATION: Cedar dugout canoes

FOOD: Fish, meat, and wild foods

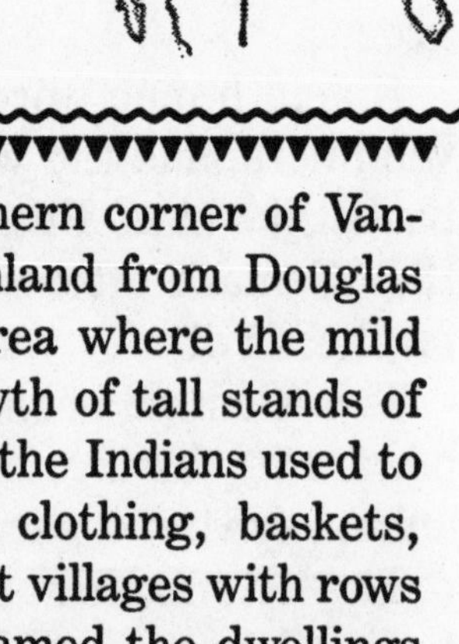

The Kwakiutl lived on the northern corner of Vancouver Island and along the mainland from Douglas Channel to Bute Inlet. It is an area where the mild rainy climate encourages the growth of tall stands of red and yellow cedar trees, which the Indians used to build their houses and to make clothing, baskets, boxes, and nets. The Kwakiutl built villages with rows of houses facing the sea. They framed the dwellings with large posts and covered them with cedar planks. In front they placed poles carved with figures representing their clan. Several families belonging to the same clan lived in each house.

The Kwakiutl depended upon salmon as their main food source, but they also caught cod and halibut on hooks or by trapping, harpooning, or netting them. They smoked most of the fish over large fires to preserve it. The men dug shellfish and hunted seals

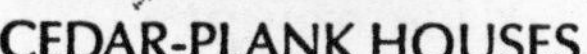

CEDAR-PLANK HOUSES

HATS, c. 1900

CARVED CEDAR CANOE

and sea lions along the coast. They went inland to hunt for deer and elk. Women went along to gather berries, roots, and other wild foods.

The Kwakiutl traveled in large, elaborately carved and painted dugout canoes made from cedar logs. Sometimes they put up skin sails when traveling from village to village.

Men usually wore no clothes; women wove cedar bark into skirts, capes, and basketlike caps. When it was cold, they wore skin shirts and wool capes woven from mountain goat or dog hair. They often oiled their cedar-bark clothing to make it waterproof. It could be woven into several layers for extra warmth.

The Kwakiutl believe in Serpent, who represents the underworld. He is also the god of wealth whose two-headed figure appears on small pieces of T-shaped copper, one in front, one in back, and a human head in the middle. Copper, a very important item of wealth among tribes of the northwest coast, was used as a ceremonial object and often given as gifts at potlatch feasts. Kwakiutl hosts sometimes gave away potlatch gifts that they had obtained on credit. Hosts borrowed items, mostly blankets, from friends and relatives and then had to pay back the lenders with 100 percent interest: two blankets in return for one.

In the late 1700s the Kwakiutl became trappers and entered the fur-trading business. Missionaries brought new religions to the area but the Indians resisted, preferring their own religious observations, including potlatches. Eventually many members of the tribe died from foreign diseases. In the 1900s the Canadian government, not understanding the importance of potlatches to every aspect of Kwakiutl life, outlawed them. The Kwakiutl, who had survived white settlement and disease, could no longer resist white domination because the last remnant of their traditional life had been outlawed.

Descendants of the Kwakiutl live in British Columbia.

MAIDU

(MY-doo)

MEANING OF NAME: Unknown

CULTURE AREA: California

LOCATION: Northeastern California

DWELLING TYPES: Conical shelters and earth lodges

CLOTHING MATERIALS: Skins and fiber

TRANSPORTATION: Cedar dugout canoes, log rafts and snowshoes

FOOD: Acorns, fish, meat, and wild plants

The Maidu lived in the high mountain meadows of northeastern California and in mountain valleys, where they collected quantities of acorns each year. They built small settlements close together, forming villages that they connected with well-worn trails. They built a ceremonial lodge in the largest and most centrally located village. Bands of Maidu who lived in the foothills built substantial earth-covered houses. Those who lived in the mountains built conical houses, which they covered with bark. When these people left their villages for prolonged periods of time, they built small temporary shelters covered with grass and twigs.

The rich resources of the area enabled them to live entirely off the land. They celebrated the first salmon run of the season by netting and spearing hundreds of spawning fish, which they dried and stored. The women collected seeds, berries, nuts, and wild plants, and the men hunted deer, elk, bear, geese, ducks, and quail all year. They particularly prized grizzly bear hides, and made them into robes to be worn during important ceremonies. The men collected wild tobacco to smoke on the same occasions.

Maidu men wore buckskin breechcloths or no clothes at all. Women wore two-sided aprons made of buckskin or of woven grass and bark, and basketlike caps. The women wore leggings and moccasins insulated with grass in winter and robes of deerskin or mountain lion

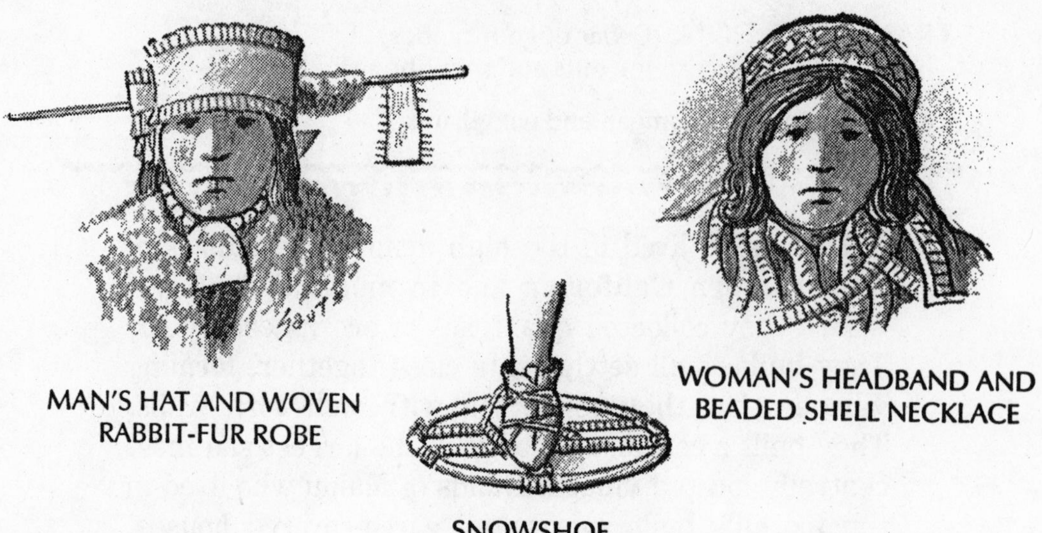

MAN'S HAT AND WOVEN RABBIT-FUR ROBE

SNOWSHOE

WOMAN'S HEADBAND AND BEADED SHELL NECKLACE

with the fur turned to the inside. The women pierced their ears and the men pierced their noses.

The Maidu believe in the Creator. Their mythology includes stories which pit Coyote, the trickster, against Earth Initiator, the Good One.

Most of the Maidu land was granted to an American settler who brought cattle into the area in 1844. The cattle destroyed most of the wild foods and many Maidu died from hunger and later from smallpox brought to the region by gold miners. Survivors ate livestock to keep from starving, but white settlers punished the Indians by hunting them down and killing them. The Maidu signed a treaty ceding their land in exchange for the safety of a reservation, but the treaty was not honored. Government soldiers forcibly marched four hundred and sixty-one Maidu to Round Valley in northern California. Thirty-two people died on the trip.

Descendants of the Maidu live in California on small reservations or in communities near the reservations.

MALISEET

(MAL-eh-seet)

MEANING OF NAME: Lazy speaker

CULTURE AREA: Northeast

LOCATION: New Brunswick, Canada, and northern Maine

DWELLING TYPES: Log houses and conical shelters

CLOTHING MATERIAL: Skins

TRANSPORTATION: Birch-bark canoes and snowshoes

FOOD: Meat, fish, and wild plants

The Maliseet lived along the Saint John River, an area where the winters are long and cold and where food sources are too limited to support a large population. They hunted, fished, and gathered wild food all year. In summer, when food sources were more plentiful, they lived in rectangular log cabins with bark roofs. Each cabin housed several related families. In the wintertime, however, they traveled in small groups and lived in single-family, conical houses covered with bark.

Meat and fish supplied them with most of their food, although some of the women planted small gardens of corn, beans, and squash near their settlements—crops which were often harvested before they had fully ripened. The Maliseet traveled to the coast each summer to dig shellfish, but the women returned to their

villages regularly to tend their gardens. In the fall the women collected roots and wild berries, especially grapes, which grew in abundance. The men hunted moose, and they took bears from their dens while they slept, honoring the animal afterwards with a ceremony.

The men wore buckskin breechcloths; the women wore buckskin skirts. In the winter they all wore leggings, moccasins, and fur robes.

The Maliseet believe that their culture hero, Gluscap, has the power to change animals into other life forms and can explain events that happen in the natural world. They tell stories from fall until spring, when the spirits are sleeping, but never during the summer.

European fur trappers convinced the Maliseet to trap for them, which altered the tribes' annual food-gathering activities and made them dependent upon European goods. White settlers moved onto Maliseet land in the late 1700s and many Indians died from contracting European diseases. In 1980 the Maliseet living in Houlton, Maine, received $900,000 from the federal government as part of an $81.5 million land settlement paid to descendants of the Passamaquoddy and Penobscot tribes.

Descendants of the Maliseet live on reservations in northern Maine and New Brunswick, and many of them are employed outside the reservation.

MANDAN

(MAN-dan)

MEANING OF NAME: Unknown

CULTURE AREA: Plains

LOCATION: North and South Dakota

DWELLING TYPES: Earth lodges and tipis

CLOTHING MATERIAL: Skins

TRANSPORTATION: Horses

FOOD: Corn, meat, and wild foods

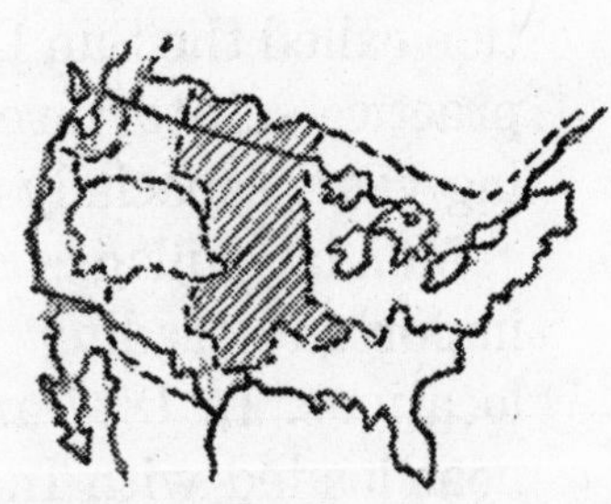

The Mandan who called themselves "men" or "people," occupied territory along the upper Missouri River on a rolling expanse of short-grass plains. Few trees or shrubs grew between the hills and dales where the Mandan built their tall, golden, earth lodges. The lodges were framed with logs and covered with earth and grass. Each lodge had a narrow entrance facing east, and was built around an open area reserved for ceremonies and special events. The Mandan built some of their villages on high bluffs above the Missouri River so they could watch for invaders. Sometimes families moved to wooded areas in the winter to hunt for deer and small animals.

The Mandan farmed in summer and hunted buffalo the rest of the year. Women planted crops of corn, beans, and squash, which they stored for winter or traded with trappers and other tribes. After their crops were planted each spring, the Mandan went buffalo hunting, leaving a few older people behind to tend the crops. When hunting, they lived in skin-covered tipis arranged in large circles.

The Mandan men wore buckskin aprons, leggings, and moccasins; the women wore one-piece buckskin dresses. They both wore buffalo-skin robes and moccasins when it was cold.

The Mandan believe everyone has four souls, which are disguised as spirits. Each year they hold a celebration called the Sun Dance. They dance, fast, feast, and practice self-torture to insure prosperity for the coming year, especially an abundance of buffalo.

Mandan villages along the Missouri River became important trading posts because of their strategic locations. In 1837 an American Fur Company steamboat loaded with Indian trade goods sailed out of St. Louis up the Missouri River. Several officers on board came down with smallpox, so the boat stopped and they were removed. The steamboat and its cargo, however, did not stop, nor was it fumigated, because the delay would cost the company too much money. The boat traveled all the way up the Missouri River carrying the disease to every Indian settlement along the way. When it returned downriver, loaded with furs, more than fifteen thousand Indians had died from smallpox. Many survivors killed themselves to avoid their sorrow and the stench of the dead. Thirty surviv-

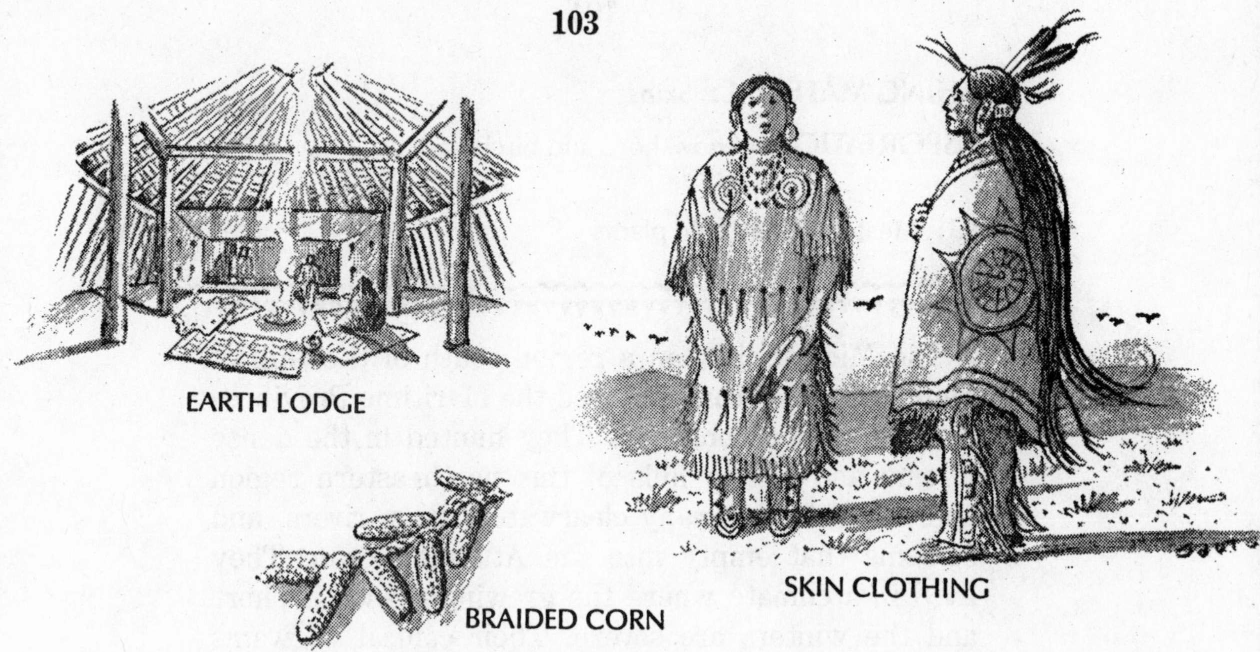

ing Mandan joined a handful of Hidatsa and Arikara and went to live on a small reservation in South Dakota. In 1948 Garrison Dam was built on part of their reservation and the best farmland, schools, homes, and cemeteries were flooded. The Mandan were moved to an area west of the newly formed Lake Sakakawea, where their descendants live today.

MICMAC
(MIK-mak)

MEANING OF NAME: A name that now means Indian

CULTURE AREA: Northeast

LOCATION: Nova Scotia and New Brunswick, Canada

DWELLING TYPE: Conical shelters

CLOTHING MATERIAL: Skins

TRANSPORTATION: Snowshoes and birch-bark canoes

FOOD: Meat, fish, and wild plants

The Micmac lived in a region south of the Gulf of Saint Lawrence that included the Maritime Provinces and the Gaspe Peninsula. They hunted in the dense forests and rolling hills of this northeastern region and fished in the many clearwater lakes, rivers, and streams that empty into the Atlantic Ocean. They lived in a climate where the growing season is short and the winters are severe. Their conical wigwams were made with young saplings covered with birch bark, skins, or mats.

The Micmac were primarily hunters and fishermen and traveled all year in small bands collecting seasonal foods. In January they went seal hunting, in February and March they stalked moose and caribou, in April and May they fished and hunted fowl, from June to September they fished for cod and collected shellfish, in September they gathered spawning eels, in October they hunted and trapped elk and beaver, and in November and December they caught a type of fish that they called ponamo, which spawns under the ice.

The Micmac men wore plain skin breechcloths; the women wore painted leather skirts. They both added fur robes and leggings made of deer or moose skin in cold weather.

In the wintertime, they strapped large square-toed snowshoes to their feet to travel over light, fluffy snow. They used smaller snowshoes when traveling over hard, crusty snow. During the rest of the year

WINTER BARK HOUSE

WOMAN'S HAT

MAN'S COAT

BIRCH-BARK CANOE

they traveled the waterways in long, narrow, lightweight birch-bark canoes that were shaped like helmets, with semicircular crests over the openings.

The Micmac believe in Gluscap, the warrior-trickster, who teaches them their arts, prophesies the future, and who will return some day.

In the 1600s the Micmac trapped for the French instead of hunting and traveling to seasonal fishing and food-gathering sites. They became so dependent upon European trade goods that trapping became their new way of life. Many Indians died from European diseases, alcoholism, and intertribal warfare. Those who survived moved to reservations in Maine and Canada, where their descendants live today.

MIWOK
(MEE-wuk)

MEANING OF NAME: Man

CULTURE AREA: California

LOCATION: Northern California

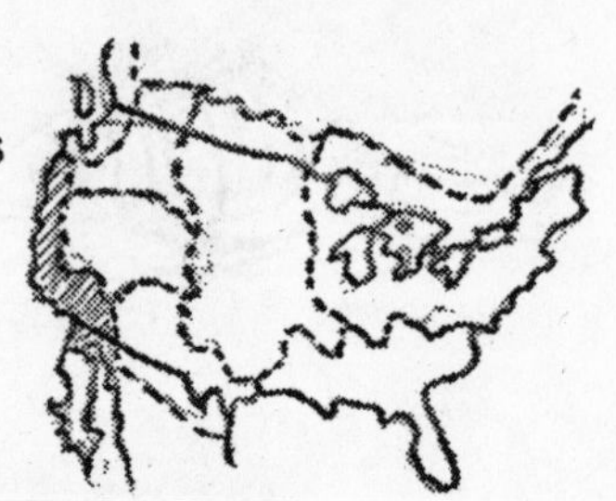

DWELLING TYPES: Conical shelters and earth lodges

CLOTHING MATERIAL: Skins

TRANSPORTATION: Unknown

FOOD: Acorns, fish, meat, and wild plants

The Miwok lived along the California coast between present-day San Francisco and Monterey, and inland to the Sierra Nevada mountains, where moist mild winds nourish coastal ranges and inland valleys. The Coast Miwok built conical houses, which they framed with forked poles and covered with grass. Their villages had ceremonial lodges similar in style to their houses, but covered with pine needles. The Inland Miwok built round houses, digging out floors below ground, framing them with poles, and covering them with grass and soil.

The Miwok obtained most of their food from the many varieties of acorns they collected each year. The firm shells of acorns makes them easy to store without any preparation. The Miwok did not plant crops, but gathered wild foods all year round. Salmon and sturgeon filled their rivers and streams, clams and mussels

abounded along the coast, and deer and elk flourished in their mountains and valleys. In many parts of the region, men collected wild tobacco to smoke on special occasions.

The men wore no clothing, but the women wore two-sided, fringed deerskin aprons. They both wore sleeveless tunics and capes woven of strips of jackrabbit fur when it was cold.

The Miwok believe that Coyote, the trickster, defeated a mythological monster who once lived in the area.

In 1794 the Spanish established a mission at San Jose and forced the Coast Miwok to work for them. Many Indians died from disease, overwork, and lack of nourishing food. The missionaries replaced the Coast Miwok with bands of Inland Miwok, who continually escaped and hid in the mountains with bands of the Yokut. For ten years the Miwok and the Yokut raided the mission for food and supplies. In 1846 American settlers came into the region and began lumbering, dairying, and farming operations on the

Indian lands. The Miwok signed a treaty ceding their land in exchange for a reservation where they would be safe. The treaty was never honored and the Miwok were forced to work for settlers or move in with neighboring tribes. Finally, in the early 1900s, the United States government purchased small parcels of the old homeland of the Miwok for reservations.

Descendants of the Miwok live on reservations in the foothills of the Sierra Nevada Mountains and in surrounding communities.

MOHAWK

(MO-hawk)

MEANING OF NAME: Man-eaters

CULTURE AREA: Northeast

LOCATION: North central New York

DWELLING TYPE: Longhouses

CLOTHING MATERIAL: Skins

TRANSPORTATION: Elm-bark canoes

FOOD: Corn, meat, fish, and wild plants

The Mohawk lived in the mid–Mohawk River Valley, which extends from Schoharie Creek to East Canada Creek. It includes a portion of upstate New York and Vermont south of the St. Lawrence River. The Mohawk built their villages on hilltops and planted large gardens in the valleys below. They lived in long,

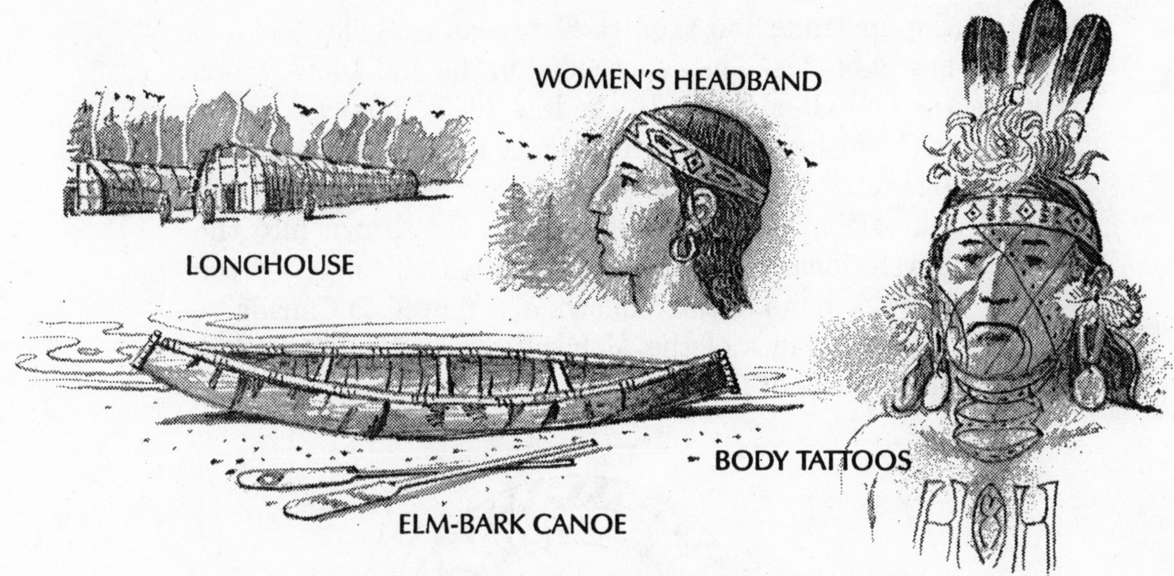

narrow houses framed with logs and covered with bark. Five or six related families lived in each house.

The Mohawk were primarily farmers who cultivated huge crops of corn, beans, and squash. Corn supplied most of their food, although the women collected many wild foods and the men went on long hunting and fishing expeditions. Mohawk women stayed in the villages and made many decisions for the tribe.

The men wore deerskin breechcloths and the women wore skirts and corn-husk slippers when it was warm. In winter, they both wore fur robes and moccasins. Mohawk men liked to tattoo their bodies with elaborate geometric designs.

Each fall the Mohawk gave thanks for their bountiful harvest by dancing, praying, and feasting.

The Mohawk belonged to the League of Six Nations, sometimes called the Iroquois Confederacy. League members referred to the Mohawk as "keepers of the eastern door."

The Mohawk fought against their Algonquian-speaking neighbors because they wanted to control the fur trade and acquire European axes, knives, and sword blades. They succeeded in the mid-1600s, when they obtained guns. In the late 1600s, however, many of the Mohawk moved to Canada and settled on the St. Lawrence River near Montreal. Others stayed in the mid–Mohawk River Valley and were drawn into the Revolutionary War by their British allies. After the war this band of the Mohawk also moved to Canada.

Descendants of the Mohawk live in Canada and in many parts of the United States.

NATCHEZ

(NATCH-iz)

MEANING OF NAME: Unknown

CULTURE AREA: Southeast

LOCATION: Mississippi

DWELLING TYPE: Rectangular thatched houses

CLOTHING MATERIAL: Fiber

TRANSPORTATION: Cypress, poplar, and pine canoes

FOOD: Corn, meat, fish, and wild plants

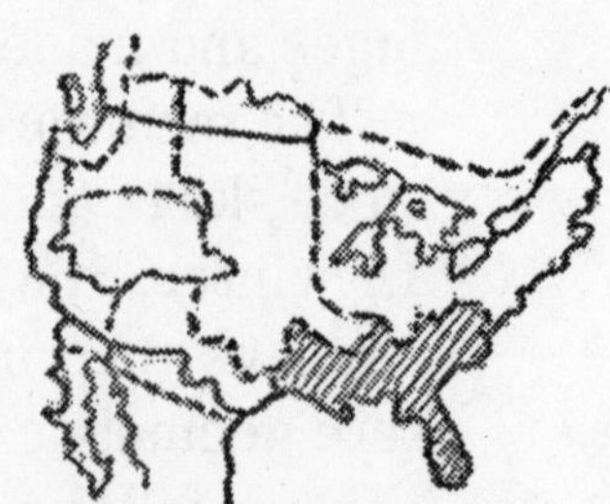

The Natchez lived in permanent villages along the banks of the Mississippi River near the present-day city of Natchez. Long periods of warm weather and abundant rainfall created the semitropical environment that allowed the Natchez to raise plentiful crops

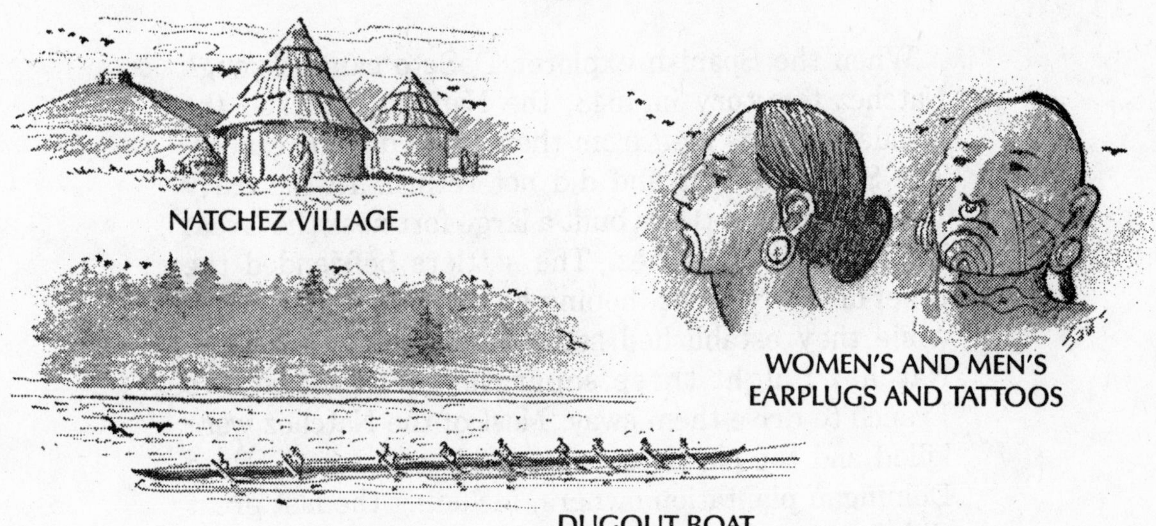
NATCHEZ VILLAGE

WOMEN'S AND MEN'S EARPLUGS AND TATTOOS

DUGOUT BOAT

and hunt numerous wild animals in nearby forests. They built their houses in a circle around a public square that was reserved for special events. They framed the houses with wood and covered them with mats or with earth. Their main village had two buildings facing each other in the public square—one a temple, the other a cabin for the Chief, or "Great Sun." The Chief inherited his position from his mother's side of the family and his duties included greeting the rising sun each morning from the temple. When he died, his wives and followers chose to die with him.

The Natchez raised corn, beans, pumpkins, and squash in their gardens, and they smoked quantities of fish, which the men caught along the banks of the Mississippi River or its tributaries.

The men wore breechcloths; the women wore skirts woven from the inner bark of mulberry trees. Men and women decorated their bodies with tattoos and paint and wore ear plugs and earrings. Believing a flat forehead to be a sign of importance, the Natchez pressed a board against their infants' foreheads when they were in the cradleboard.

When the Spanish explorer DeSoto came through Natchez territory in 1543, the Natchez attacked the invader and his men from their large dugout canoes. The Spaniards left and did not return. In the early 1700s, French settlers built a large fort near the Great Village of the Natchez. The settlers befriended the Chief of the Natchez, hoping he would maintain peace while they established settlements nearby. But the Natchez fought three separate wars against the French to drive them away. Most of the Natchez were killed and the survivors were sold as slaves to Santo Domingan plantation owners, including the last great Chief among them. Some Natchez escaped and went to live with the Creek, Cherokee, and Chickasaw.

Descendants of the Natchez live among the Oklahoma Cherokee.

NAVAJO

(NAV-eh-ho)

MEANING OF NAME: Large field

CULTURE AREA: Southwest

LOCATION: New Mexico and Arizona

DWELLING TYPE: Domed round houses

CLOTHING MATERIALS: Cotton and fiber

TRANSPORTATION: Horses

FOOD: Corn, meat, and wild plants

The Navajo lived west and south of the Chama Valley, an arid desert inhospitable to trees and animals. The Navajo came from the north in the early 1500s, roaming the deserts and mountains, raiding other tribes, gathering wild foods, hunting, and fishing. They built dome-shaped round houses, which they called hogans, at the base of cliffs or in canyons. They made trips into the mountains to fell piñon pine trees to frame their hogans, which they covered with mud and clay. Hogans were built far apart because food sources (and, later, grazing lands) were spread over a wide area. When it was very hot, some families left their hogans and moved into temporary open shelters that they made by imbedding forked timbers into the ground and covering the roof with sage and desert brush, leaving the sides open.

The Navajo planted small gardens and traveled long distances to hunt and gather nuts, fruits, and seeds. Because one of their legendary ancestors had promised to turn himself into a fish, the Navajo gave up eating fish. They became successful sheepherders and breeders after the Spanish had brought sheep and goats to the region.

Navajo men wore woven yucca breechcloths; women wore short skirts woven of the same material. They both wore sandals, leggings, and woven yucca blankets. The Hopi taught them how to weave cotton and wool, and they used it to replace their woven-fiber clothing. Women often wore handwoven rectangular pieces of cloth, called mantas, tied over their shoulders and around their waists. In the late 1800s women wore long cotton and rayon skirts and velveteen blouses like those worn by European women. Men wore white cotton pants and velveteen shirts. The Navajo learned that Pendleton Mills in Oregon made

WINTER HOGAN SUMMER SHELTER

WOMEN'S CLOTHING

MEN'S CLOTHING

NAVAJO COMMUNITY COLLEGE, c. 1975

blankets by machine, so in 1890 they began to wrap themselves in Pendleton blankets. The men preferred plain blankets; the women liked them fringed. They sold their handwoven blankets to tourists and traders.

The Navajo believe that they emerged from lower worlds. They borrowed many traditions from their Pueblo neighbors, including masked dancing, sand painting, and the use of cornmeal and pollen for religious observances.

Horses, first used for raiding, became an important means of transportation for the Navajo. When a man died, his horse and saddle were often buried with him.

The Navajo joined the Pueblo Revolt of 1680 in an effort to drive the Spanish from the Southwest. Later they moved to Arizona and settled near the Hopi. They became farmers and herdsmen, but they continued to raid Spanish settlements. In the mid-1800s, when New Mexico became part of the United States, they were forced to move to a reservation. Many refused to leave their homeland, so the United States Government commissioned Kit Carson to move them. He starved them off the land by killing their livestock and burning their crops. Survivors walked over three hundred miles from Fort Defiance, in Arizona, to Fort Sumner, in central New Mexico. Two thousand Indians died from the march and the stifling confinement at Bosque Redondo reservation. It was too small to accommodate the many tribes living there, the soil was too poor to support crops, there was no game, and the government did not send the provisions promised. Government officials finally decided to move the Navajo to a large piece of arid wasteland in Arizona and New Mexico. When the Allotment Act was passed in 1887, the land occupied by the Navajo was so undesirable that white settlers did not fight to settle on it or to have it divided. For over a hundred years the Navajo have successfully coaxed life out of their desert environment, feeding their bodies and minds in spite of many deprivations. Some of the land they have lived on for many years belongs to their neighbors, the Hopi, many of whom want it back. It is currently in dispute.

Tribes of the Navajo live in Arizona and New Mexico.

NEZ PERCE

(nez-pehr-SAY)

MEANING OF NAME: Pierced noses

CULTURE AREA: Plateau

LOCATION: Idaho, northeastern Oregon, and southeastern Washington

DWELLING TYPES: Rectangular A-shaped houses and tipis

CLOTHING MATERIALS: Fiber and skins

TRANSPORTATION: Snowshoes and wooden dugout canoes

FOOD: Roots, fish, meat, and wild plants

The Nez Perce Indians lived in the lush basin of the Columbia River. It is a region of fast-flowing rivers, tall mountains, and fertile valleys. Moisture-laden air tumbles in from the Pacific Ocean encouraging luxuriant plant growth. In the valleys, wild blue hyacinths flourish; spawning salmon fill the Columbia River and its tributaries; and deer, elk, moose, and bear feed freely in the nearby Bitterroot Mountains. These plentiful food resources enabled the Nez Perce to live off the land all year round. They built their semipermanent villages in sheltered areas near a good source of water. Their long, narrow, A-shaped communal houses were framed with poles and covered with mats. Every village had a chief, who assigned each clan or band a place to live and another place where they could fish. Camas roots, which are the bulbs of wild hyacinth plants, supplied the Nez Perce with most of their food and were dug twice a year, dried, and stored for the winter. Some bands traveled annually to the plains to hunt buffalo, building temporary skin-covered tipis with the floors dug below ground. The Nez Perce created a special pemmican recipe using bone marrow and dried buffalo meat, but it did not contain berries. They believed marrow gave their pemmican more texture and was a better fat source.

Nez Perce men and women wore woven-fiber clothing before they adopted skin clothing. Men wore breechcloths, shirts, moccasins, and leggings made of deer, elk, and buffalo skins. Women wore long buckskin dresses, moccasins, leggings, and woven, pointed fez-style hats with feathers and tassels. They both wrapped themselves in fur blankets when it was cold. Nez Perce women were expert tanners and prepared beautiful buffalo hides for clothing and tipi covers. Their skins were traded, along with sheep horns, to tribes on the lower Columbia River. Formal clothing was often fringed along the seams and elaborately decorated with beads, quills, and paint in geometric designs.

The Nez Perce traveled in winter on oval snowshoes made of wood and elk hide. They used dugout canoes the rest of the year. The men built their canoes with

MAT-COVERED LONGHOUSE AND SKIN TIPI

SHEEP-HORN SPOON

WOMEN'S CLOTHING AND WOVEN BAG, c. 1850

MAN'S HAT

vertical sides and flat bottoms, using driftwood logs, which they collected along river banks. They steered them with crudely carved poles.

The Nez Perce enjoy a very simple, free, religious life with few ceremonies. They believe that spirits, especially Coyote, the hero-trickster, live in trees, hills, rivers, and in other natural objects. Coyote and his helpers deliver people from the monsters. To honor their spirits, the Nez Perce dance, feast, and pray each year.

In the mid-1800s the Nez Perce fought against tribes from the plains to keep them away from their fur-trapping territory. Christian missionaries came to the region later and permanently divided the tribe. Those who adopted Christianity signed a treaty ceding to the government all tribal land except the small part they lived on. The traditionalists, led by Chief Joseph and White Bird, rejected the treaty and refused to leave their land. They fought valiantly, but in the end they were forced to flee. They were captured while trying to escape into Canada, and government soldiers took them to a reservation in Indian Territory. Many died before being allowed to return to their homeland. In later years their reservation land was reduced in size so that white settlers could buy the land. By the early 1900s, many members of the tribe had died from European disease.

Descendants of the Nez Perce live on a reservation in Idaho, where some of them practice traditional customs. The land is mostly leased to white farmers and ranchers.

NOOTKA

(NOOT-keh)

MEANING OF NAME: Unknown

CULTURE AREA: Northwest

LOCATION: Vancouver Island, British Columbia

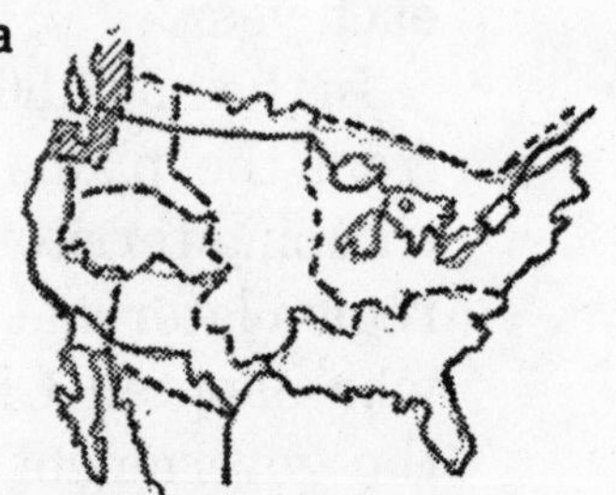

DWELLING TYPE: Plank houses

CLOTHING MATERIAL: Bark

TRANSPORTATION: Cedar dugout canoes

FOOD: Fish, meat, and wild plants

The Nootka lived on the west coast of Vancouver Island, which was formed thousands of years ago when part of the Coast Range became submerged beneath the sea. The island has a steep, rocky coastline and is covered with a dense cedar forest. The forests provided the Nootkas with their greatest source of natural materials and allowed some of their men to become expert woodworkers. They built large peaked-roof houses, framed them with timbers, and covered them with cedar planks. The planks belonged to individual families and were taken along when families camped at summer fishing or hunting sites. Cedar posts inside the houses portrayed carved animal figures representing the clan living in the house. Several related families lived in each house.

For their main food source, the Nootka depended on several varieties of salmon. They also enjoyed halibut and herring, and preserved the fish by smoking it over large fires. The men were expert whale hunters and took their cedar canoes far out into the Pacific Ocean to harpoon the giant mammals. The village chief, the only person who could afford a whaling boat and a crew, was usually the harpooner, an extremely dangerous job. The chief employed highly organized helpers, whom he trained himself. When not out whaling, the men hunted seals, sea lions, and ducks along the coast, and deer, elk and small animals inland.

The men usually wore no clothing, but the women wore short, two-sided, yellow cedar-bark skirts, and hats woven of spruce root. In cold weather the men wrapped themselves in cedar-bark robes that went under the left arm and were pinned over the right shoulder, leaving both arms free. Women wore robes that covered their shoulders and had sleeves to the elbows. When it rained they often added a triangular waterproof cape. Some chiefs wore bearskin robes when they went whaling. An elongated head was a sign of prestige for the Nootka, who bound the heads of young children to make them cone shaped.

The Nootka believe in Sky-God, and that the universe is filled with spirits. They employ medicine men who inherit their spiritual knowledge from relatives, but who must be trained by other medicine men to perform healing rituals. Like other northwestern tribes, the Nootka displayed their importance by hosting extravagant potlatch parties.

European trappers came to the island to hunt sea otters, but few white settlers came, because the soil and the weather did not favor farming. During the 1800s the Nootka caught dogfish and harpooned basking sharks for their liver oil. Even though dogfish oil was a good native food, it was saved to trade with

settlers on the mainland in exchange for blankets, metal tools, food, and European clothing. The oil was good for lubricating European saw-mill machinery and fueling lamps. They did not trade whale or seal oil because it was too tasty. In the late 1800s and early 1900s, the Nootka began to hunt seals in the Bering Sea because seal skins became more profitable than dogfish oil. Fog and storms along the coast made this a very dangerous activity, which few tribes would attempt. By 1911, however, seals became almost extinct in the region, and by International agreement seal hunting was ended.

European diseases and alcohol killed many of the Nootka. Missionary zealots did everything in their power to stop the survivors from practicing their traditional religion, including outlawing the use of medicine men and potlatches. Other new laws prohibited the Indians from fishing along their traditional rivers and streams and from gathering cedar bark, because logging companies owned most of the forests.

When schools and industries began to flourish on the island, the Nootka were moved to reservations. The Canadian government, not understanding the social, religious, and economic implications of potlatches, outlawed these parties even on the reservations. Except for small tracts of land, such as Victoria Harbour, British Columbia, the natives never surrendered their land by treaty. Despite talk about settling this question, Canada continues to expand its parks system along the western coast into Indian lands.

Descendants of the Nootka live on reservations on Vancouver Island, British Columbia, and in the state of Washington, in the United States.

NORTHERN SHOSHONE and BANNOCK

(sho-SHO-nee and BAHN-ehk)

MEANING OF NAME: Unknown

CULTURE AREA: Western Plateau

LOCATION: Idaho

DWELLING TYPES: Tipis and conical huts

CLOTHING MATERIAL: Skins

TRANSPORTATION: Horses, bullboats, dugout and birch-bark canoes

FOOD: Meat, fish, and wild plants

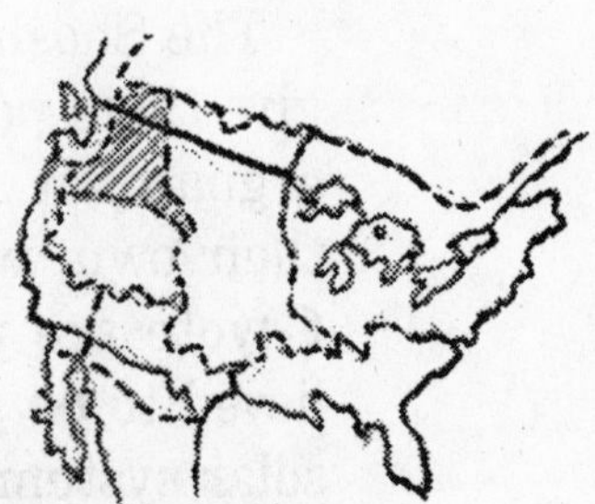

The Northern Shoshone and Bannock Indians who called themselves "nimi" or "the people," lived south of the Salmon River in Idaho. They hunted in the

nearby Bitterroot Mountains and fished in the Salmon and Snake rivers. The Northern Shoshone were related to other Shoshone Indians living to the south and east. The Bannock were a Northern Paiute band from Oregon. At some time in the past, the Northern Shoshone and Bannock joined together and became one tribe. They lived in skin-covered tipis and conical grass huts and traveled in small organized groups.

The Northern Shoshone and Bannock caught large quantities of fish, particularly salmon, upon which they depended. They supplemented their diet with wild plants and roots and the meat of deer, elk, and mountain sheep. Some bands traveled afar to hunt buffalo in the Lemhi Valley, on the upper Snake River plains, and in Montana and Wyoming.

The Shoshone acquired horses in the early 1700s, and some groups rode them long distances to hunt buffalo. Those who owned only a few horses seldom used them for hunting.

The men wore leather breechcloths, leggings, and shirts; the women wore leather dresses. They both wore moccasins and fur robes. Indians who did not hunt buffalo wore clothing made of rabbit skin and sage bark.

The Shoshone believe in spirits who guide them and give them power to cure the sick. They are guided by a guardian spirit who gives each of them a song of their own, which they sing in time of need. Wolf and Coyote are popular mythological figures. Wolf is believed to be good because he created humans and the solar system. Coyote is believed to be bad because he opposes Wolf and brings disorder to the world.

The Shoshone have a long tradition of ceremonial dancing that begins in the spring, when they dance the Circle Dance to celebrate the first salmon of the

SKIN TIPI AND GRASS HOUSE

STONE-DISC PIPE

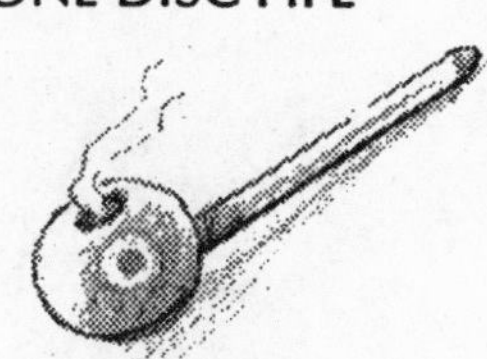

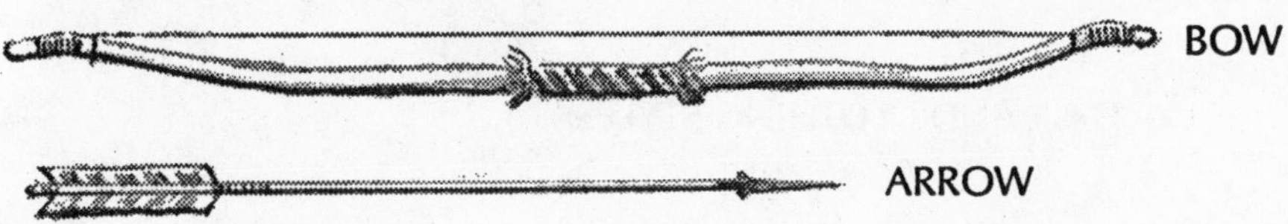

BOW

ARROW

season. They also dance the Bear Dance, Rabbit Dance (done only by men), and Scalp Dance (done mostly by women).

Early in the 1800s the homeland of the Northern Shoshone and Bannock was invaded by fur traders, who set up trading posts on the Snake River and traded utensils and weapons for beaver and other animal skins. The arrangement worked well until white settlers moved onto the land in the 1860s. In 1863, after several clashes, soldiers from Fort Douglas, Utah, massacred several hundred Indians who were camped on the Bear River. Fifteen years later, starving Indian survivors warred against the settlers, who would not allow the Indians to gather camas roots.

The Fort Hall Reservation, near Pocatello, Idaho, was established in 1867, and shortly thereafter the Boise and Bruneau Shoshone came to live there. In 1868 the Fort Hall Shoshone and Bannock joined them, and in 1907 the Lemhi and Sheepeater Shoshone came to live on the reservation. These four groups of Sho-

HAIR AND CLOTHING STYLES

shone are called the Fort Hall or Northern Shoshone. The reservation was greatly reduced in size by the opening of mines, the coming of the Union Pacific Railroad, and the settling of the town of Pocatello, Idaho. What remained was later divided between the natives and the white settlers. Tribal members received parcels of land and the government sold the remaining land to white settlers.

Descendants of the Northern Shoshone and Bannock live on the Fort Hall Reservation in Montana, where they farm and ranch.

OMAHA

(O-meh-haw)

MEANING OF NAME: Those going against the mind or the current

CULTURE AREA: Plains

LOCATION: Northeastern Nebraska

DWELLING TYPES: Earth lodges and tipis

CLOTHING MATERIAL: Skins

TRANSPORTATION: Skin bullboats

FOOD: Meat, corn, and wild plants

The Omaha lived in the rich, broad valley of the Missouri River—a valley cut by ancient glaciers that left behind large deposits of fertile soil. Indian gardens in the region were productive, and buffalo herds came to feed on the tall, green grass. It was natural for the Omaha to exploit their resources both by cultivating crops and by buffalo hunting. Their homes were large, round, earth lodges framed with logs and covered with branches, grass, and sod. They planted their gardens near their villages and used nearby bluffs to keep a lookout for enemy invaders. After planting their crops in the spring, they went buffalo hunting and lived in skin-covered tipis arranged around an open area on the plains. Each clan was assigned a special place within the circle, and the opening was reserved for sacred ceremonies.

Buffalo meat supplied the Omaha with most of their

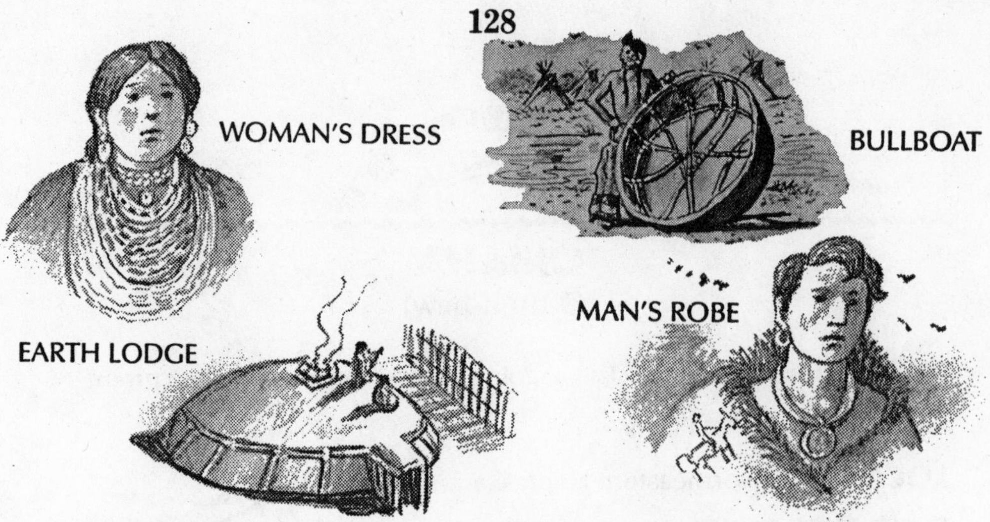

food, and corn, beans, and squash supplemented their diet. The men also hunted elk, deer, and small animals in the winter when there was no more grass to attract the buffalo.

Men wore buckskin aprons, leggings, and moccasins; women wore sleeveless leather dresses fringed at the sides. They both wore buckskin robes in cold weather. They tattooed their bodies with elaborate designs, which they considered a sign of wealth. Men often gained prestige by having their daughters tattooed with a small black circle in the center of their foreheads to represent the sun, and a four-pointed star on their chests to symbolize the night.

The Omaha believe in Wakan Tanka, an invisible force that controls all living events. They also believe that spirits travel along the Milky Way to visit the dead.

In the early 1800s over three hundred Omaha died from European diseases, a result of their contacts with white traders. Survivors were made to cede their land to settlers and move to a reservation in Nebraska. Government officials later sold a portion of this land to the Winnebago and eventually divided it even further. Members of both tribes received parcels of land

and the rest was sold to white settlers. Alice C. Fletcher, a well-known ethnologist, who helped the Omaha fight for their rights in the late 1800s, persuaded Congress to give them citizenship status, legal title to their parcels of land, and protection from white squatters. Many Omaha kept their land, but others sold it or were duped into selling it by white settlers.

Descendants of the Omaha live on or near a reservation in Nebraska.

ONEIDA
(o-NY-deh)

MEANING OF NAME: People of the stone setup

CULTURE AREA: Northeast

LOCATION: North central New York

DWELLING TYPE: Longhouses

CLOTHING MATERIAL: Skins

TRANSPORTATION: Birch-bark canoes

FOOD: Corn, meat, fish, and wild plants

The Oneida lived along the frigid, fast-moving waters of Oneida Creek, which flow into Oneida Lake in central New York. They fished the lake and creek and hunted as far north as the St. Lawrence River. At the time of European contact they lived in large palisaded villages, each containing nearly one hundred barrel-

shaped longhouses. The houses were framed with saplings covered with bark. Animal effigies painted on the outside identified the clan that lived inside.

The Oneida grew most of their food—corn, beans, and squash—in large gardens. The men went on long hunting and fishing trips, staying away from their villages for lengthy periods of time. As a result, Oneida women made many important decisions for the tribe.

Men wore deerskin breechcloths; women wore short skirts. They both added moccasins and fur capes when it was cold.

The Oneida believe in friendly spirits, ritual curing of diseases, and herbal medicine.

One of the smallest of the Iroquois tribes, the Oneida replenished their population by adopting members of other tribes, including captives. At various times in their history, one-half of them were Algonquian-speaking people. They belonged to the League of Six Nations, the Iroquois Confederacy.

Throughout the 1600s and 1700s the Iroquois Confederacy warred against neighboring tribes in an effort to control the fur trade. The Oneida traded with the British, who supplied them with high-quality goods in exchange for furs.

The Revolutionary War permanently divided the Iroquois tribes because the Oneida and Tuscarora voted to side with the Americans, while the others chose to side with the British. The split caused a civil war among the tribes. After the war the council chiefs voted to put out the council fires—ending a united Iroquois Confederacy.

In 1779 General George Washington convinced the pro-American Oneida to join his company in an attack against tribes of the Onondaga, Cayuga, and Seneca. Although victorious, the Oneida were made to cede most of their land and watch as American troops burned their villages. White settlers later took most of their remaining land and many Indians moved onto a reservation near Niagara Falls. Plagued by famine, they moved back to Lake Oneida to fish, hunt, and plant crops with tribal members who had remained in their homeland. The two groups did not get along well, however, and many of them eventually moved to Ontario, Canada. Others, who had become Christianized by American settlers, purchased land from the Menominee Indians and moved to Wisconsin.

Descendants of the Oneida live in Wisconsin, New York, and Canada.

ONONDAGA

(ahn-ehn-DAW-geh)

MEANING OF NAME: On top of the hill or mountain

CULTURE AREA: Northeast

LOCATION: North central New York

DWELLING TYPE: Longhouses

CLOTHING MATERIAL: Skins

TRANSPORTATION: Birch-bark canoes

FOOD: Corn, meat, wild plants

The Onondaga, who were members of the Iroquois Confederacy, lived in a beautiful secluded valley between Lake Cazenovia and Onondaga Creek in central New York, where the men caught eels in the fast-moving waters. They hunted in the surrounding hills as far north as Lake Ontario and fished in the many rivers, streams, and lakes of the region. Women gathered wild foods and planted gardens each spring. The Onondaga lived in a village only until food sources and firewood ran out; then they moved. Sometimes they palisaded their villages for protection. They built barrel-shaped, multi-family longhouses framed of thick saplings and covered with bark. Several related families shared each house.

Onondaga women harvested corn, beans, and squash each fall and preserved these vegetables for winter use. The men went on long fishing and hunting

trips. Like many Indian women, the Onondaga women made important tribal decisions.

Men wore deerskin breechcloths, and women wore short skirts, both adding moccasins and fur capes when it was cold.

The Onondaga believe in Ha-Wah-Ne-U, Creator of the World. Each new year they hold a four-day celebration called the Midwinter Ceremony, when they thank the spirits for a bountiful harvest.

Because they were a small tribe, the Onondaga added to their population by adopting captives. Other members of the Iroquois Confederacy referred to the Onondaga as "keepers of the fire" because they were centrally located and their territory became the location for council meetings. The French built missions in Onondaga territory and some of the Indians became Christians, which divided the tribe. Tribe members continued to trade with the British, whose trade goods they preferred. During the Revolutionary War, most members of the tribe sided with the British. Afterwards many fled to Canada, where they established a new league and returned to their old way of life. Others went to live on the American side of Niagara Falls.

Descendants of the Onondaga live on reservations in Canada and in New York State.

OSAGE

(o-SAYJ)

MEANING OF NAME: Unknown

CULTURE AREA: Plains

LOCATION: Western Missouri

DWELLING TYPES: Mat- or bark-covered round houses

CLOTHING MATERIAL: Skins

TRANSPORTATION: Horses

FOOD: Meat, corn, and wild plants

The Osage lived in western Missouri amid rolling hills and freshwater streams. Fertile valley soils encouraged large gardens and the growth of tall grass, which attracted herds of hungry buffalo. Buffalo meat supplied most of their food, although their gardens provided corn, beans, squash, and pumpkins. In spring, after the gardens were planted, the Osage hunted buffalo on the open prairie, and deer, turkey, and small animals wherever they made camp.

The Osage Indians built oval-shaped homes with

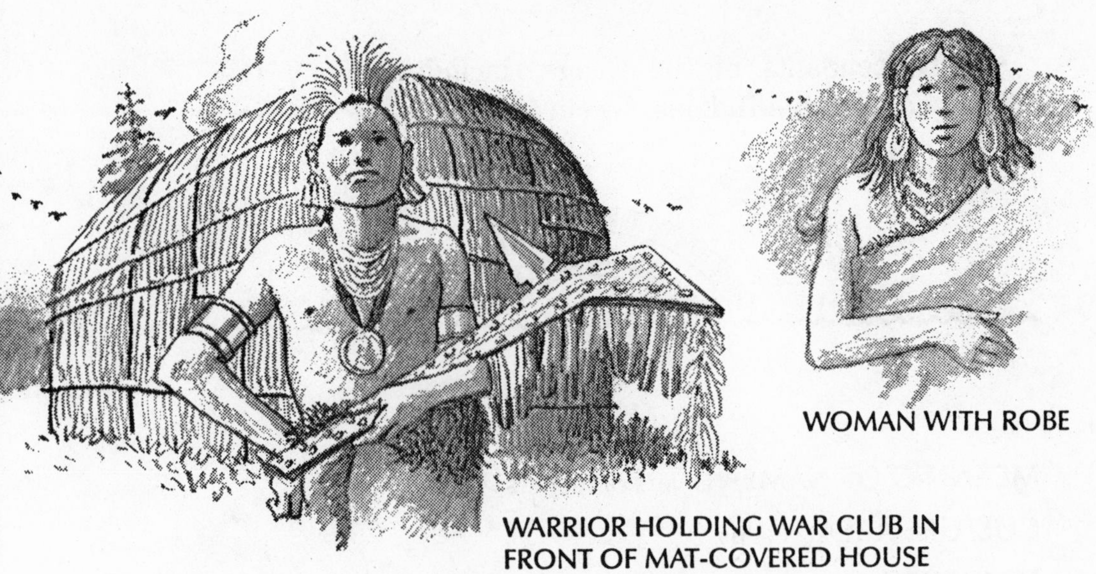

WOMAN WITH ROBE

WARRIOR HOLDING WAR CLUB IN FRONT OF MAT-COVERED HOUSE

arched poles and covered them with bark or mats. The men wore buckskin breechcloths; the women wore one-piece dresses. They both wrapped themselves in fur capes and blankets in cold weather.

The Osage believe that Wakan Tanka, the Great Force, maintains order in the sky, and that Grandfather, the Sun, taught them to make bows of osage wood and arrows as straight as the rays of the sun.

The Osage trapped deer and beaver for the French in exchange for trade goods, but they had to fight against the Ponca and Pawnee, who also wanted to trap in the region. In the 1800s they were forced to cede their territory and move to a reservation in Indian Territory. Tribe members later received parcels of land when their reservation was divided so that white settlers could buy land. Some tribe members sold their land to white settlers but kept the mineral rights. When oil was discovered on this land in the 1920s, Indian owners were paid for the drilling rights. These oil leases have allowed many tribal members to become economically independent.

Descendants of the Osage, including many full-blooded Osage Indians, live in Oklahoma.

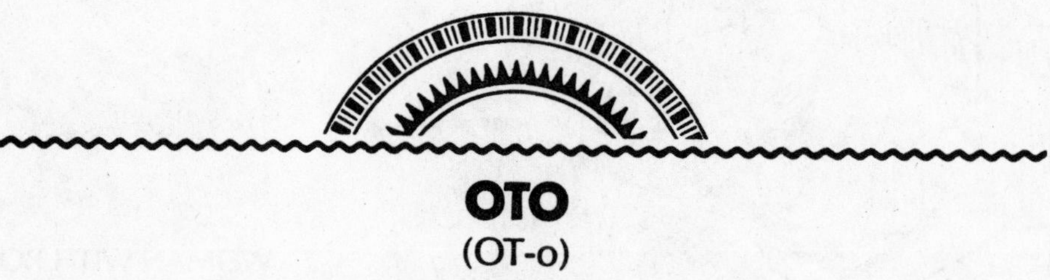

OTO
(OT-o)

MEANING OF NAME: Lovers or lechers

CULTURE AREA: Plains

LOCATION: Eastern Nebraska

DWELLING TYPE: Earth lodges

CLOTHING MATERIAL: Skins

TRANSPORTATION: Horses

FOOD: Corn, meat, and wild plants

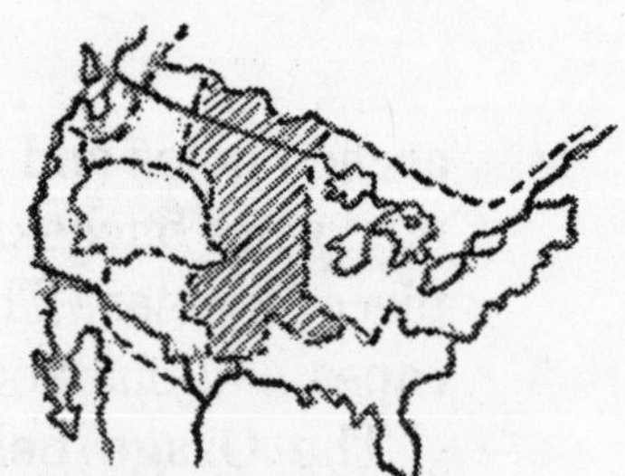

The Oto lived along the Missouri River in eastern Nebraska, where tall grasses attracted herds of buffalo and rich valley soils supported large cultivated gardens. The Oto took advantage of their environment by spending half of their time gardening and the other half hunting buffalo. They built large villages which held as many as fifty round earth lodges. They dug them several feet below ground, framed them with logs, and covered them with brush, grass, and earth. When they went hunting, they lived in portable skin-covered tipis.

Because the Oto depended equally upon both buffalo meat and preserved corn, they planted their gardens in the spring before they went buffalo hunting. Older

CARVED DRUM-SUPPORTS

HORSE AND TRAVOIS

BEAR-CLAW NECKLACE AND EAR ORNAMENTS

men and women of the tribe stayed in the village to tend the crops. Buffalo hunting was an important communal event accompanied by many sacred ceremonies. The men also hunted elk, deer, and small animals because the women preferred to make clothing out of these very fine skins. The Oto hunted on horseback and sometimes attached a travois to haul their belongings across the plains when they moved camp.

Oto men wore buckskin breechcloths and moccasins; the women wore one-piece dresses that were often decorated with snail shells. They both wore buffalo-skin robes and blankets in winter. Their formal clothing was usually decorated with snail shells.

The Oto believe that Wakan Tanka, their most important spirit, is in charge of the entire spiritual world.

The Oto lost many people from disease and warfare. In 1829 they adopted a hundred homeless Missouri

Indians. For ten years they fought against neighboring tribes and wrestled with cholera epidemics and starvation. They signed four separate treaties ceding their lands, and finally, some of them moved to a reservation between Kansas and Nebraska. Later reservation land was divided; some of it went to tribal members, the rest was sold to white settlers. In 1955 the United States Government awarded members of the Oto-Missouri tribe one million dollars for illegal land-taking.

Descendants of the Oto-Missouri Indians live in Oklahoma, where they teach their children their native language in tribal schools.

PAPAGO

(PA-peh-go)

MEANING OF NAME: Bean people

CULTURE AREA: Southwest

LOCATION: Arizona

DWELLING TYPE: Brush and earth lodges

CLOTHING MATERIALS: Skins and cotton

TRANSPORTATION: Unknown

FOOD: Corn, wild plants, and meat

The Papago lived in a portion of the Sonoran Desert south of the Gila River in present-day Arizona. Their land is surrounded by lush mountains and valleys with

freshwater springs and abundant plant life. The Papago built their villages in the foothills and along freshwater streams. They preferred to dig the floors of their round houses below ground, frame them with poles, and cover them with brush and earth. They built a Rain House in the center of some of their villages, reserving it for ceremonial events.

The Papago planted corn, beans, and squash. Corn supplied most of their food and they used it for trade with other tribes in exchange for dried meat, salt, and colored pigments. Women gathered desert fruits and seeds while the men hunted deer, antelope, and small animals.

The men wore cotton shirts and pants and the women wore cotton dresses. They both wore buckskin moccasins.

The Papago believe that when they die their souls go eastward to the land of the dead. Earthmaker is their supreme god.

The Spanish established a mission among the Papago in the late 1600s. It was raided for almost a hundred years by Apache bands, some of whom joined the Papago in the late 1800s. Ranchers later settled on the most fertile land and forced the Papago to move to the Gila Bend Reservation, an arid, useless piece of desert nearby.

Today some Papago live on reservations in southern Arizona and New Mexico; others live in local desert communities.

PAWNEE

(paw-NEE)

MEANING OF NAME: Horn
CULTURE AREA: Plains
LOCATION: Nebraska
DWELLING TYPE: Earth lodges
CLOTHING MATERIAL: Skins
TRANSPORTATION: Horses
FOOD: Corn, meat, and wild plants

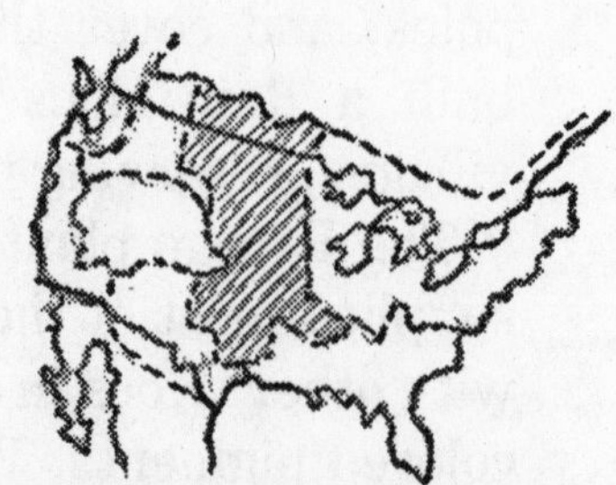

The Pawnee lived along the broad, shallow waters of the Platte River, which picks up the Loup and Elkhorn Rivers as it travels across the present-day state of Nebraska. River valley soils support fertile gardens and natural stands of tall green grass. The Pawnee built villages fortified with four-foot mounds of earth and deep trenches. The fortifications were made by digging trenches around the villages and

piling up the excavated soil in mounds. They built round earth lodges for homes, framed them with logs, and covered them with branches, grass, and earth. They spent half their time tending gardens outside the village and the other half following herds of buffalo.

The Pawnee raised two crops of corn, beans, and squash each year—one in spring, and one in late summer. Corn supplied nearly half their food needs and buffalo meat provided the rest. Buffalo hunting, which was highly organized, required the participation of all the able men in the tribe, and was always preceded by sacred ceremonies.

Pawnee men wore buckskin aprons, leggings, and moccasins; women wore buckskin skirts and capes. They both added heavy buffalo-skin robes in winter.

The Pawnee believe in a spirit father named Tirawa.

The Apache and Illinois Indians captured many Pawnee women and children during the 1600s and sold them as slaves. The Pawnee did not encounter trappers or traders until the mid 1700s because their settlements were isolated. They later contracted cholera from Whites, and many of them died. They were forced to cede their lands in the early 1800s and move to a reservation in Indian Territory, which was later reduced in size so that White settlers could buy Indian land.

Descendants of the Pawnee live in Oklahoma.

PEQUOT

(PEE-kwaht)

MEANING OF NAME: Destroyers

CULTURE AREA: Northeast

LOCATION: Central Connecticut

DWELLING TYPE: Longhouses

CLOTHING MATERIAL: Skins

TRANSPORTATION: Birch-bark and pine canoes

FOOD: Corn, meat, fish, and wild plants

The Pequot lived along a flat, narrow, coastal plain adjacent to the Connecticut River Valley. They fished in the sheltered harbors of the Thames River, planted large gardens in the fertile valley, and hunted in the nearby hills. It is not known if the Pequot always palisaded their villages, but in 1637 at least one group lived in a large palisaded village in Mystic, Connecticut, possibly to prevent other tribes from invading

their village. They built bark-covered longhouses framed with poles and arranged them around a public square.

Corn supplied them with most of their food, although they also raised beans and squash. The men raised tobacco to smoke during important ceremonies. Men hunted deer, bear, and small animals, and in the fall they hunted migrating waterfowl.

Men wore buckskin breechcloths; women wore leather skirts. They both added leggings, moccasins, and fur robes when it was cold.

The Dutch and the British both wanted Pequot land, which the Indians refused to surrender. Looking for an excuse to fight, Massachusetts Bay colonists sent troops into Pequot territory to avenge the death of two settlers who were killed by Indians, but not necessarily by the Pequot. Before the Pequot could defend themselves, many of them were massacred. The troops continued to attack and burn Pequot villages with the help of their allies, the Narragansett, Niantic, and Mohegan, until most of the Pequot were killed. Captives were sold as slaves in Bermuda or turned over to Indian allies as repayment for their help.

Descendants of the Pequot live in or near two small reservations in Connecticut. In 1983 members of the Mashantucket Reservation there were granted federal recognition and awarded $600,000 to acquire land and $300,000 for economic development.

PONCA

(PAHN-keh)

MEANING OF NAME: Unknown
CULTURE AREA: Plains
LOCATION: Northeastern Nebraska
DWELLING TYPES: Earth lodges and tipis
CLOTHING MATERIAL: Skins
TRANSPORTATION: Horses
FOOD: Meat, corn, and wild plants

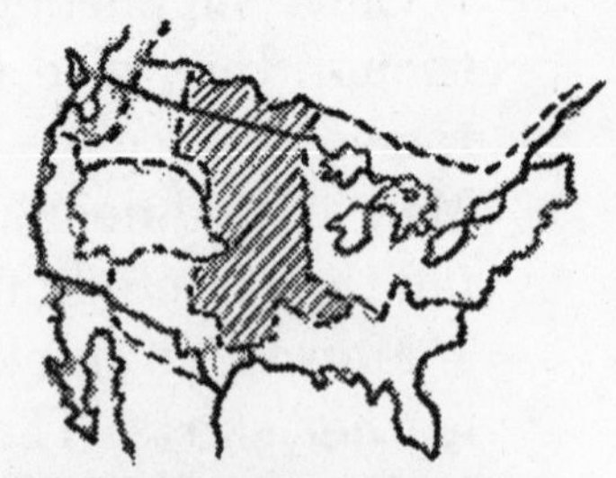

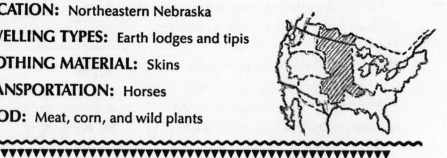

The Ponca lived in the rich lowlands of the Missouri River Valley, which was filled with luxuriant tall grass. The grass attracted herds of buffalo, and the prairie soils supported large crops of corn. The Ponca were able to divide their time between farming and hunting buffalo. They built large earth lodges with foundations dug below ground. They framed these lodges with logs and covered them with brush and earth. Sometimes they built high walls of earth around their villages, using soil excavated from deep trenches that were left in front of the walls.

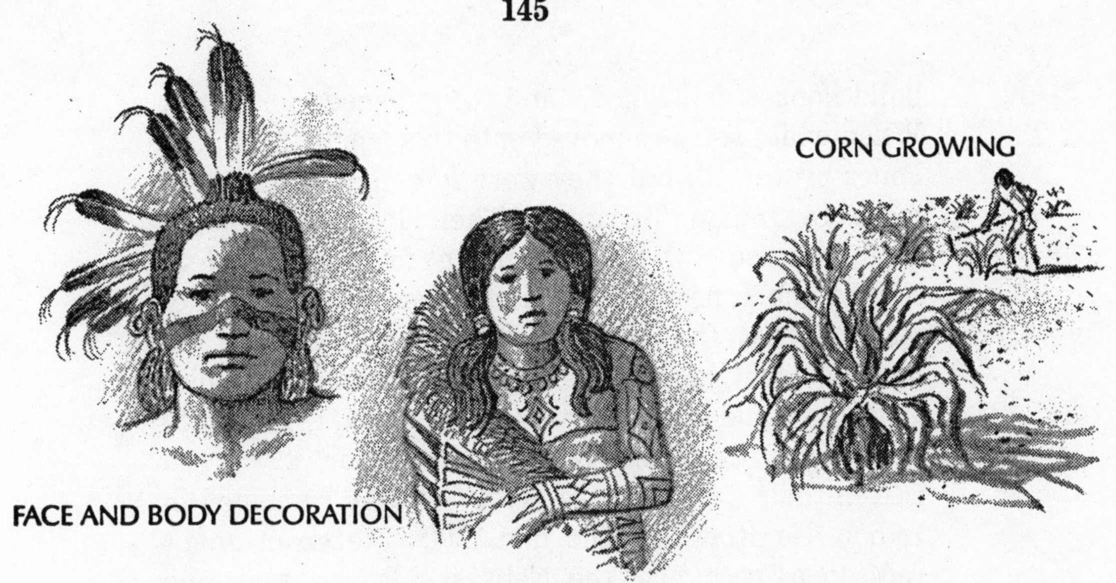

The Ponca planted gardens of corn, beans, and tobacco each spring. When they went buffalo hunting, they set up skin-covered tipis in large circles on the prairie. Within the circle each clan was assigned a particular location; the center was reserved for sacred ceremonies, which preceded each hunt. The Ponca drove the buffalo to their deaths over cliffs or chased them on horseback and shot them with bows and arrows.

The men wore breechcloths, shirts, and moccasins; the women wore short aprons or one-piece leather dresses, which they decorated with floral and geometric designs done in quills and beads. When it was cold they both added leggings, fur robes, and blankets.

The Ponca smoke the sacred pipe each year during their annual celebration of the Pipe Dance. They worship Wankan Tanka, who is their Great Spirit.

The Ponca sold most of their land to white settlers in the mid-1800s, keeping only a very small parcel to live on. Five years after the sale, they received partial payment for the land, but by then many of them had died of starvation. The survivors used the money to build houses and schools and to buy seeds for crops. When white settlers moved onto this land in 1876, the Ponca protested, but they were forced at gunpoint to move to Indian Territory. Their leader, Standing Bear, pleaded with the government for help. His pleas stirred the conscience of many Americans, who demanded that the government review the case and make a legal judgement regarding land ownership. The court ruled in favor of the Ponca who returned to their Nebraska farms. For many, however, it was too late in their lives to move again, so they remained in Indian Territory. In the mid-1900s the government refused to recognize the Nebraska Ponca as a tribe because they did not meet certain government requirements.

Descendants of the Ponca live in Oklahoma and Nebraska.

POTAWATOMI

(pahteh-WAHTEH-mee)

MEANING OF NAME: Person or Indian

CULTURE AREA: Northeast

LOCATION: Southern Michigan

DWELLING TYPE: Bark- or mat-covered wigwams

CLOTHING MATERIAL: Skins

TRANSPORTATION: Wooden dugout or elm-, linden-, and birch-bark canoes

FOOD: Corn, meat, fish, and wild plants

The Potawatomi lived in the lower peninsula of Michigan where they fished along the southern coast of Lake Michigan and hunted westward into the interior forests of Wisconsin. It was a region with abundant and diverse food sources, which they exploited all year. They hunted bear, deer, elk, buffalo, and smaller animals in the winter and fished most of the year. They also ate dogs, although mostly for ritual purposes. They built large summer villages at the edge of the forest near prairie grassland and freshwater streams. Their dome-shaped dwellings, called wigwams, were framed with saplings and covered with bark or mats. Sometimes three generations of related families lived in one house. In winter the Potawatomi broke up into small bands and moved to sheltered valleys. Some moved to open prairie in the summer to hunt buffalo.

Corn supplied the Potawatomi with most of their food, although fish and animal meat were very important. In mid-April they set up camps in dense maple groves and collected sap. They boiled it down into syrup and sugar and used it to flavor their food. Men cultivated tobacco to use for special occasions.

Men wore deerskin leggings and breechcloths decorated with porcupine quills and beads; women wore long, sleeveless, deerskin dresses belted at the waist. Both wore deerskin moccasins.

The Potawatomi believe that Chibiabos gave them tobacco and corn, and that Kegangizi, the water mon-

MAT-COVERED LODGE

YOUNG HUNTER

YOUNG WOMAN FORMALLY DRESSED

ster, is responsible for evil deeds. They believe each person has a spirit of his own called a Manitou.

The Potawatomi fought against both the French and the English in the 1700s. They lost their land through a series of broken treaties and were forced to move to Indian Territory. Some refused to go and others fled to Canada. The United States government assigned troops to forcibly move them to Oklahoma but the soldiers did not know the way and they left the Potawatomi in Missouri, Kansas, and Iowa. The Potawatomi rebuilt their farms and villages wherever they were left, but a few years later they were rounded up again and moved to Indian Territory. Their reservation was later divided and most of it was sold to white settlers.

Descendants of the Potawatomi live in Wisconsin, Michigan, and Ontario, Canada.

QUINAULT

(quin-AWLT)

MEANING OF NAME: Unknown

CULTURE AREA: Northwest

LOCATION: Washington

DWELLING TYPE: Plank houses

CLOTHING MATERIALS: Fiber and skins

TRANSPORTATION: Cedar dugout canoes

FOOD: Fish, meat, and wild plants

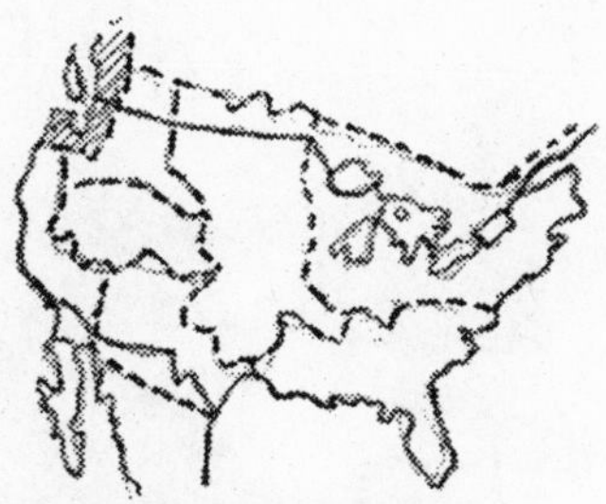

The Quinault lived along the Quinault River on the Pacific Coast side of the Olympic Peninsula. Warm ocean currents create mild year-round temperatures there which encourage lush evergreen forests and the abundant growth of berries, roots, and greens. The Quinault built large, gable-roofed houses, which they framed with posts and covered with cedar planks. Many had large porches in front, where the men worked and socialized. Ten or twelve families belonging to the same clan shared each house.

The Quinault depended upon several varieties of salmon as their main food source. They netted it, harpooned it, or caught it on single lines. They also caught trout, halibut, cod, sole, and herring. Some clans went whaling in ocean-going canoes and also hunted sea otters, sea lions, and seals along the coast.

They also dug for shellfish. Inland, the men hunted elk, bear, and deer.

The men wore no clothes; the women wore grass and bark skirts. They both wore blankets woven of rabbitskin or doghair, cedar-bark hats, and rain capes. When the men went hunting, they wore skin moccasins and leggings.

The Quinault believe in guardian spirits, daily bath-

FAMILY AT MEALTIME

ing, fasting, and physical exercise. Clans and groups displayed their wealth and social position by hosting extravagant potlatch parties.

Their isolated homeland kept the Quinault out of contact with Europeans until the late 1800s. When white trappers entered their territory, many Indians caught smallpox and died. The survivors ceded all but a small bit of land, which was later enlarged and made into a reservation. In 1963 the Quinault and the neighboring Queet received $205,000 for land settlement claims against the United States government.

Descendants of the Quinault live on a reservation in Washington State where they run a lumber mill, a salmon hatchery, and a fish-processing plant. Some of them live in the towns of Taholah and Queets and make their living primarily from the sea.

SAN JUAN

(san-WAHN)

MEANING OF NAME: San Juan Bautista

CULTURE AREA: Southwest

LOCATION: New Mexico

DWELLING TYPE: Multifamily adobe houses

CLOTHING MATERIAL: Fiber and cotton

TRANSPORTATION: Unknown

FOOD: Corn, meat, and wild plants

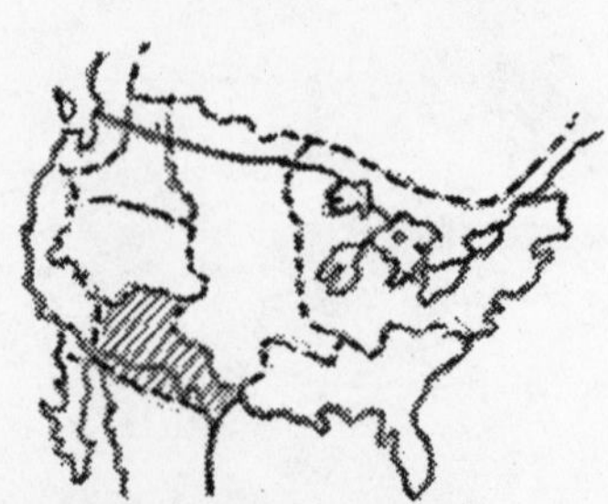

The San Juan settled north of present-day Santa Fe, New Mexico, on the eastern bank of the Rio Grande River, where they have lived for almost five hundred years. Warm year-round temperatures, ample water sources, and a fertile floodplain fill the valley between the Rio Grande and Rio Chama rivers, where the Indians planted large gardens. To the north, high

mountains abound with wild game and plants. The San Juan live in five-story houses made of sun-dried adobe bricks, and which are connected in rows like apartment houses. The living quarters for each family are separated by a terrace, which forms the roof of the house beneath. The San Juan Indians are often called the Pueblo, which is the Spanish word for village.

San Juan men planted and tended large gardens of corn, beans, and squash. Corn supplied most of their food, while deer and rabbits provided them with meat.

The men wore woven breechcloths, shirts, belts, and leggings, and the women wore one-piece woven dresses. They both wore buckskin moccasins.

The San Juan built large, round ceremonial chambers, called kivas, dug below the ground and entered by way of a long ladder. The kivas were reserved for sacred events. The San Juan used two kivas—one during the summer, the other during the winter. They believe in rain and cloud gods and teach their children to impersonate these gods by dancing while wearing masks. Many children are initiated into the Ohuwa

Society, which teaches them about sacred ceremonies.

The Spanish established a settlement among the San Juan in 1598, but it failed because its administrator spent too much time plundering other settlements in the Southwest looking for gold. A succession of Spanish leaders worked the San Juan people very hard, burned their kivas and their sacred objects, and deprived them of their religious freedom. When the Spanish jailed a group of Indian religious leaders, including a San Juan man, natives throughout the southwest revolted and drove the Spanish out. It was called the Pueblo Revolt of 1680. Twelve years later, when the Spanish returned, they treated the natives more kindly. One-third of the San Juan Indians died during a severe smallpox epidemic.

Descendants of the San Juan still live in their ancient pueblo in their traditional lifestyle.

SEMINOLE

(SEM-eh-nol)

MEANING OF NAME: Separatist or runaway

CULTURE AREA: Southeast

LOCATION: Florida Everglades

DWELLING TYPE: Thatched-roof houses

CLOTHING MATERIALS: Skins and cloth

TRANSPORTATION: Cypress dugout canoes

FOOD: Corn, fish, meat, and wild plants

The Seminole lived deep in the Florida Everglades, a dense saw-grass marsh that looks like an innocent, placid grassland without trees. The hot year-round temperatures, broad shallow basin waters, and lime-rich soils cause rapid plant decay, which encourages the saw-grass growth. The Seminole adapted to their hot swampy environment. They built settlements of open-sided houses with thatched roofs, placing them high above the ground on stilts to keep them dry. A separate house in the middle of each settlement was reserved for cooking and eating meals.

Seminole women raised corn, beans, squash, and tobacco wherever the land was dry. They collected grapes, figs, plums, and other fruits. Men hunted deer, bear, and other animals, and fished all year round.

The Seminole were a mixture of Native American Indians—runaway Yamasee, Oconee, and Creek—and black slaves who had escaped from their owners. The Spanish named the group "Seminole," the Creek word for runaways. The Seminole fought their first major war in 1817 in an attempt to stop illegal raiders from coming down from the north to capture black slaves. In 1819, when Florida became part of the United States, the Seminole were ordered onto a reservation. They refused to move. Under the leadership of several warriors, including Osceola, Wild Cat, and Alligator, they fought against removal for nearly sixteen years. Eventually over three thousand Seminole were forcibly moved to Indian Territory. Some escaped into the Florida Everglades and were chased by government troops because settlers wanted the Blacks for slaves. The chase became too costly, however, and the government finally gave up.

The Seminole settled on reservations in Florida,

MAN'S CLOTHING
WOMAN'S CLOTHING
THATCHED-ROOF
HOUSE
TURKEY-FEATHER FAN
MAN POLING DUGOUT BOAT
THROUGH EVERGLADES

where the women obtained sewing machines and developed colorful European-style clothes by sewing together scraps of imported cotton.

Descendants of the Seminole live on reservations in central Florida and in Oklahoma.

SENECA

(SEN-i-keh)

MEANING OF NAME: People of the big hill

CULTURE AREA: Northeast

LOCATION: North central New York

DWELLING TYPE: Longhouses

CLOTHING MATERIAL: Skins

TRANSPORTATION: Snowshoes and birch-bark canoes

FOOD: Corn, meat, fish, and wild plants

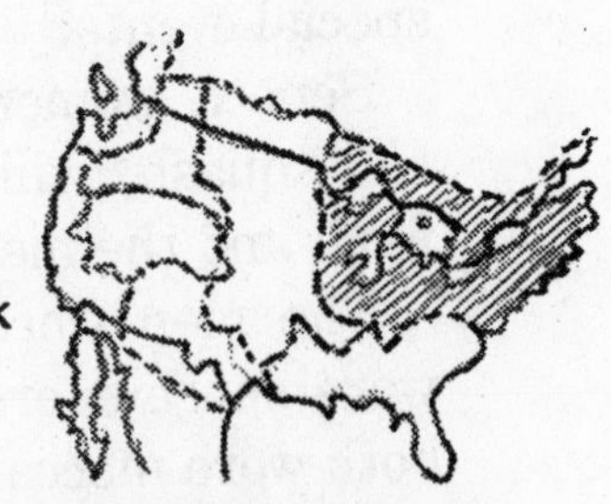

The Seneca lived between the Genesee River and Canandaigua Lake in New York State in a valley where rich soil supported abundant animal and plant life. The Indians fished and hunted as far north as Lake Ontario and eastward to the highlands between Seneca and Cayuga lakes. As the single largest tribe of the Iroquois Confederacy, they protected the other tribes from attack from the west and south. They built barrel-shaped longhouses framed with thick saplings and covered with elm bark. Between fifty and sixty

clansmen lived in each house. The houses were arranged around a Council House that was reserved for special events.

Seneca women cultivated gardens of corn, beans, and squash, which supplied them with most of their food, and the men hunted and fished all year.

The men wore deerskin breechcloths; the women wore short deerskin skirts. In the wintertime, they both wore moccasins and fur capes.

The Seneca believe in spirits, particularly in one called Earth Holder. Their most sacred event is the Midwinter Ceremony, which takes place each winter and lasts for eight days. Members of the False Face Society come at that time wearing grotesquely carved wooden masks. Their purpose is to heal the sick.

The Seneca belonged to the League of Six Nations, the Iroquois Confederacy, and were called "keepers of the western door." Throughout the 1600s and 1700s the Seneca fought against the French and neighboring tribes in an effort to control the fur trade. When the western Seneca began trading with the French, the tribe became divided in its loyalty between the French and British. The Seneca tried to remain neutral during the American Revolution, but the British convinced them to fight as their allies. After the war American soldiers destroyed Seneca villages, and many of the Indians moved to Canada, while others stayed in their homeland. They were later forced to cede their New York lands and move to Kansas. Some Seneca moved, but others remained. Eventually the latter group was given reservation land in New York State.

Descendants of the Seneca live on several reservations in New York State and in Ontario, Canada.

TETON
(TEE-tahn)

MEANING OF NAME: Dwellers on the prairie

CULTURE AREA: Plains

LOCATION: South Dakota, southeastern Montana, and northwestern Nebraska

DWELLING TYPE: Tipis

CLOTHING MATERIAL: Skins

TRANSPORTATION: Horses

FOOD: Meat and wild plants

The Teton settled near the Black Hills of South Dakota after they left their old homeland near the

Great Lakes. The tall, rocky peaks of the Black Hills extend over one hundred miles from north to south. Deer, elk, and bear fed in the forests, and buffalo came to feed on the adjacent tall-grass prairie. The Tetons, often called the Western Dakota, followed migrating herds of buffalo most of the year. Each spring they moved from sheltered canyons onto the prairie and set up their skin-covered tipis in large circles. Men organized communal buffalo hunts and held sacred ceremonies before each hunt to honor the animals.

Buffalo meat supplied the Teton with most of their food. They used the rest of the animal for clothing, tipi covers, tools, and utensils. They drove buffalo herds over cliffs or surrounded them with grass fires.

The men wore buckskin breechcloths; women wore one-piece belted dresses and moccasins. In cold weather they both added leggings and buffalo robes. Men wore feathered headdresses to show they had performed a brave deed.

The deity called Wakan Tanka is regarded as a supreme force to the Teton, who employ shamans and priests to interpret their dreams and visions and to conduct rituals and herbal cures for diseases. A celebration called the Sun Dance is held each summer during which the Teton fast, feast, dance, and practice self-torture.

The Teton are one of three major subgroups of the Sioux Indians. The other two are the Yankton and the Santee. When the wagon trains crisscrossed Teton lands, destroying the grass and driving away the buffalo, the Teton allied themselves with several other Indian tribes to keep the settlers out. They fought for almost half a century to keep their lands and signed several treaties, which were never honored. In 1868

Red Cloud, a chief of the Oglala band of the Teton, accepted reservation land in western South Dakota and moved there with his people. The nearby Black Hills were sacred to the Teton, who went there to worship. When gold was discovered in the hills, the Teton were forbidden to go into the hills to worship. Later their reservation was divided into five smaller reservations to make room for other homeless Indians. In the late 1800s the Teton began to hold a celebration called the Ghost Dance with the hope that these celebrations would, through supernatural means, bring an end to the white settlers, who were taking Indian land and destroying the environment.

Descendants of the Teton live on several small reservations in South Dakota.

TLINGIT

(CLING-git)

MEANING OF NAME: People

CULTURE AREA: Northwest

LOCATION: Southeastern Alaska

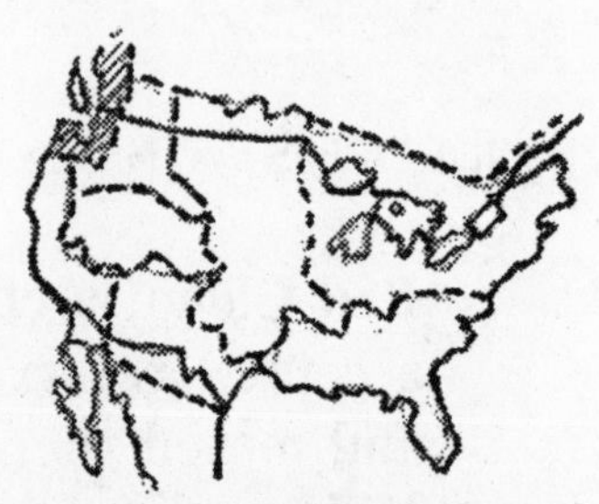

DWELLING TYPE: Plank houses

CLOTHING MATERIALS: Bark and skins

TRANSPORTATION: Spruce and cedar dugout canoes

FOOD: Fish, meat, and wild plants

The Tlingit lived along the Alaskan coastline from Mount St. Elias to the Portland Canal. Being a region of rugged fiords, Tlingit villages, like most Indian villages along the coast, could be reached only by sea travel. Dense spruce forests flourished in the mild, damp climate, and native woods supplied the Indians with materials for their houses, clothing, and household utensils. Their favorite wood, however—red and yellow cedar—did not grow in the region, so they traded furs for it. The Tlingit built rectangular houses framed with large posts and covered with spruce and cedar planks. They lined them in rows along sandy beaches near salmon streams. Inside the houses, the center posts were carved with clan figures. Several related families lived in each house. The Northern Tlingit belonged to the Eagle Clan and the Southern

Tlingit belonged to the Wolf Clan. They both carved small posts to honor the dead and placed them in front of their houses. Later they traded with skilled Haida craftsmen who carved large cedar posts (often called totems) for them. Many of these posts still stand today.

The Tlingit depended on fish as their primary food source. They caught quantities of halibut, salmon, herring, and candlefish. They also hunted seals, sea lions, and sea otters along the coast. Inland they sought deer, bear, mountain goats, and small animals. They traded copper and sea otter skins for shells and slaves. Most Northwest Coast Indians ranked tribal members according to the importance of their lineage. Indians belonging to the least important families were considered low-class and were often traded for material possessions.

The Tlingit men wore no clothing, but the women wore woven cedar-bark skirts. Both wore basketlike hats, some trimmed with sea otter fur. They oiled their clothing to make it waterproof, but it was so light it dried quickly even if not oiled. Men wore seal and deerskin leggings and moccasins in the northern part of the territory.

The Tlingit built large dugout canoes of Sitka spruce logs. They also traded with the Haida for their expertly crafted red cedar canoes.

The Tlingit employ shamans to cure the sick and to accompany war parties. It is believed their hero-trickster, Raven, stole the Sun, the Moon, and the stars and gave them to the Tlingit. The Tlingit displayed their wealth and social status by hosting extravagant potlatch parties.

The Tlingit fought against Russian fur trappers who established a trading post in the region in the 1700s. The Russians sailed into Tlingit harbors and took Indian women and children as hostages; they gave the Tlingit men traps, demanding furs in return for the hostages. In the early 1800s many Tlingit died from smallpox. The United States bought Alaska from Russia in 1867 and shortly thereafter began to lease river and stream rights to commercial fishing and canning companies, who stopped the Tlingit from fishing in their native villages.

Descendants of the Tlingit live in Alaska.

TONKAWA

(TAHN-keh-weh)

MEANING OF NAME: They all stay together

CULTURE AREA: Plains

LOCATION: Central and south Texas

DWELLING TYPES: Tipis and conical shelters

CLOTHING MATERIAL: Skins

TRANSPORTATION: Horses

FOOD: Meat, wild plants, and fish

The Tonkawa lived in the broad valleys of the Brazos and Red rivers in Texas. They traveled in small bands and roamed all year in search of food. Their nomadic lifestyle required portable housing, so they built their homes in two styles: short, squat skin-covered tipis, and conical shelters framed with poles and covered with twigs and grass.

The Tonkawa tracked buffalo over a wide area, but they stayed out of Comanche territory to the west and north. Besides buffalo, they hunted deer and bear, and also fished and gathered wild foods. They roasted buffalo and deer meat over an open fire and pounded it into pemmican, which they traded with other tribes for corn.

The men wore long buckskin breechcloths, moccasins, leggings, and shirts; the women wore short buckskin skirts. They both added thick buffalo robes in

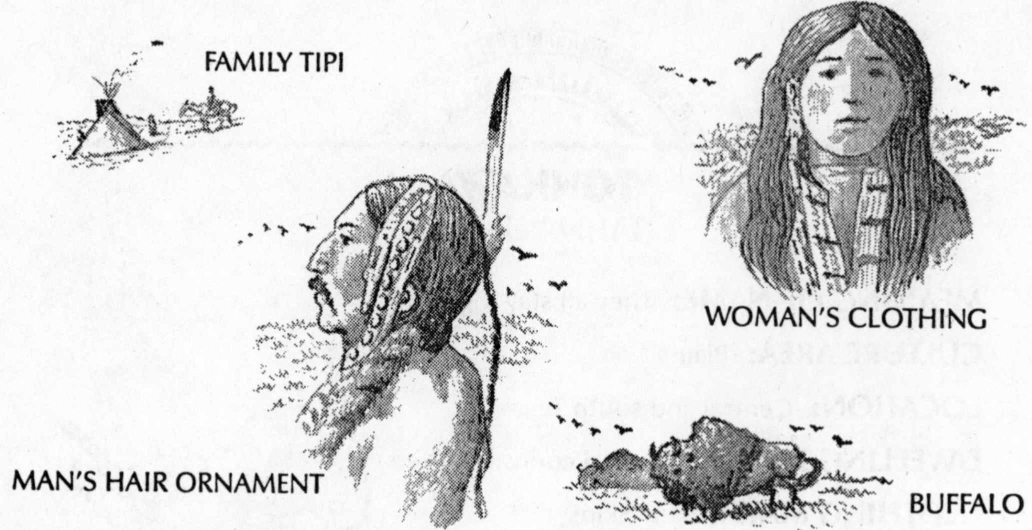

cold weather. They liked to decorate their bodies with paint and tattoos.

The Tonkawa believe spirits belong to the dead and that owls and wolves represent important spirits and should never be killed.

American soldiers encouraged the Tonkawa to join them in their battles against the Comanche, but when the fighting ended, the Tonkawa were still made to cede their land and move to a reservation in Kansas. The Tonkawa were later moved to another reservation in Indian Territory. In 1862 this reservation was attacked by an unknown enemy and most of the Tonkawa were killed. The attack, coupled with an epidemic of smallpox, left few survivors. The embittered survivors later became successful raiders, who terrorized settlers in central and northern Texas for ten years in retaliation for their shabby treatment. The Tonkawa eventually joined tribes of the Lipan and moved to a reservation in Iowa, but later they moved back to Indian territory.

Descendants of the Tonkawa live in Oklahoma.

TSIMSHIAN

(SIM-she-an)

MEANING OF NAME: People of the Skeena River

CULTURE AREA: Northwest

LOCATION: British Columbia, Canada

DWELLING TYPE: Plank houses

CLOTHING MATERIALS: Bark and skins

TRANSPORTATION: Snowshoes, log rafts, cedar dugout and bark canoes

FOOD: Fish, meat, and wild plants

The Tsimshian lived along the banks of the Skeena, Niska, and Nass rivers in southwestern British Columbia, where fish spawned, edible roots grew in abundance, and wild animals flourished. Clans living along the Nass River developed a monopoly on candlefish oil because these fish were abundant in that river. They traded the oil with the Tlingits, who lived north of them, and with the Kwakiutl, who lived south of them. They also took the oil overland to trade it for furs with inland tribes. They built large gabled, multifamily houses, which they framed with posts and covered with cedar planks. Several families belonging to the same clan lived in each house. They often carved the interior posts of their houses with animal and human figures, some of which represented their clans.

Fish supplied the Tsimshian with most of their food.

CEDAR-PLANK HOUSE

MAN'S DANCE CLOTHING

They caught several varieties of salmon, codfish, candlefish, halibut, and herring. The men hunted seals and sea lions along the coast. Inland they hunted mountain goats, bear, and deer. They traded their candlefish oil to the Haida for sea otters, large canoes, and totem poles; to the Tlingit for copper; and to the Kwakiutl for slaves and dentalia, or tusk shells, that were found in deep waters on the seaward side of Vancouver Island.

Tsimshian men usually wore no clothing, but the women wore woven cedar-bark skirts. Men and women both wore woven cedar-bark capes, which they oiled to make waterproof. When it was cold they added fur robes or cedar-bark capes woven in layers to make them warm. They also wore tall, pointed, basketlike hats woven of cedar bark and grass. Tsimshian women wove Chilkat blankets of cedar bark and mountain goat wool.

The Tsimshian traveled on snowshoes in the colder northern reaches of their territory, and in small dugout canoes, lightweight bark canoes, and flat rafts in the southern part of their territory. They preferred the large cedar dugout canoes made by the Haida, who were expert canoe builders.

Tsimshian mythology includes stories about spirits and supernatural beings, especially Raven, the trickster. They believe in a supreme Sky-God. In the wintertime, Tsimshian clans and groups displayed their wealth and status at potlatch parties. The wealthiest clans and families gave gifts of copper, shell, and woven blankets.

When the Hudson Bay Company opened a trading post in the area in the 1800s, the Tsimshian began to trap for the white settlers in exchange for trade goods. Many of the Indians moved close to the trading post to make trading easier. Some of the Tsimshian later traveled to Alaska with a missionary to establish a settlement there, which later became a reservation. Those who stayed in British Columbia continued to make their living from the sea.

Some descendants of the Tsimshian live on Annette Island in Alaska, and some are in small local settlements along the coast and along inland rivers.

TUSCARORA

(tusk-eh-ROR-eh)

MEANING OF NAME: Hemp gatherers

CULTURE AREA: Northeast

LOCATION: North central New York

DWELLING TYPE: Longhouses

CLOTHING MATERIALS: Fiber, skins, and feathers

TRANSPORTATION: Birch-bark canoes

FOOD: Corn, fish, meat, and wild plants

The Tuscarora shared the fresh waters of Oneida Lake and its environs with their neighbors, the Oneida. After they had been driven from their homeland in North Carolina in the 1700s, the Iroquois Confederacy voted to give them land near Oneida Lake and invited them to join their confederacy. They built multifamily, bark-covered longhouses and planted gardens of corn, beans, and squash, being quick to adopt the customs of their Iroquois neighbors. The men fished and hunted throughout the region, and the women and children gathered wild foods.

Tuscarora men wore buckskin breechcloths held up with a woven-fiber belt; the women wore short leather skirts. In cold weather they both added moccasins, fur robes, or robes made of woven feathers. Some wore woven-fiber capes, which they had brought with them from the south.

The Tuscarora left their homes in North Carolina because white settlers had taken their land and their children and sold the children into slavery in the Caribbean. During the Revolutionary War, the Tuscarora, along with the Oneida, sided with the Americans and were attacked by other members of the Iroquois Confederacy. After the war some of them went to live in Canada, while others stayed in New York State. Still others of the Tuscarora tribe returned to North Carolina and submitted an appeal to the state legislature for payment for the land they had lost. They won their appeal and used the settlement money to pur-

CORN GRINDING　MAN'S HAT　WOMAN'S CLOTHING

chase land from the Seneca near Niagara Falls. Tuscarora descendants remain there today.

UTE
(YOOT)

MEANING OF NAME: Utah

CULTURE AREA: Great Basin

LOCATION: Western Colorado and eastern Utah

DWELLING TYPE: Conical shelters, round houses, and tipis

CLOTHING MATERIALS: Fiber, bark, and skins

TRANSPORTATION: Unknown

FOOD: Meat, fish, and wild plants

Bands of the Ute lived west of the Rocky Mountains in an area of desert sagebrush. They were organized into small family groups who hunted, fished, and gathered wild plants all year. They often built conical shelters that they covered with brush and bark. Western bands and one eastern band built permanent, dome-shaped houses—often eight feet in diameter—covered with willow boughs. When they went hunting on the Great Plains, they built skin-covered tipis.

The Western Ute caught quantities of fish; eastern bands hunted buffalo; southern bands gathered wild seeds and plants. Most bands hunted sheep, deer, elk, antelope, moose, rabbits, and buffalo whenever possible. They also dried crickets and grasshoppers and mixed them with berries to make desert fruitcake, a food that stored well. They also collected wild tobacco wherever they found it growing.

The Western Ute, who had very few animal skins, made aprons and poncholike shirts of fiber or bark. The eastern bands, who had a variety of animal skins, made leather breechcloths, leggings, and shirts for the men and long dresses for the women. They decorated their clothing with beads, shells, elk teeth, and paint. They also wore robes of rabbit skin or buffalo fur. Some of the men wore hard-soled moccasins and stockings woven out of sagebrush.

The Ute believe that all living things require some supernatural force to exist. Their shamans—both male and female—were employed to appease the spirits.

Eastern bands of the Ute came in contact with Spanish explorers in the 1600s, almost 100 years before western bands met the Spaniards. Southern and Eastern Ute bands stole horses from the Spanish and became expert horsemen. They raided their pueblo

MAN'S CLOTHING
BUFFALO
WOMAN'S CLOTHING

neighbors for food, and they captured women and children from the Western Shoshone and Southern Paiute to sell to the Spanish in New Mexico. Mormon settlers moved onto land belonging to western bands of the Ute in 1800, forcing them to move to a reservation in Colorado. Their reservation was later divided, and tribal members received parcels of land. The United States Government sold the remaining land to white settlers.

In 1950 the Utes won a $31 million lawsuit against the United States Government for land taken but not paid for. They divided the money among all bands of the Ute.

Descendants of the Ute live on a reservation along the southern border of Colorado, where they lease oil and gas rights, raise cattle, and cater to tourists.

WAMPANOAG

(wahm-peh-NO-ag)

MEANING OF NAME: Eastern or coastal people

CULTURE AREA: Northeast

LOCATION: Southeastern Massachusetts and the islands of Martha's Vineyard and Nantucket

DWELLING TYPE: Mat-covered wigwams

CLOTHING MATERIAL: Skins

TRANSPORTATION: Pine dugout canoes

FOOD: Corn, meat, fish, and wild plants

The Wampanoag lived on coastal land from Cape Cod to Narragansett Bay and on the islands of Martha's Vineyard and Nantucket. Along the coast there are broad, sandy beaches and a rich, flat, coastal plain with mountains only a short distance away. The Wampanoag built their villages near the coastline and along rivers and streams that emptied into the sea. They built dome-shaped wigwams, called witus, which they framed with saplings and covered with mats sewed of cattail leaves. They clustered their dwellings around an open space which they reserved for ceremonies and public activities.

Each spring Wampanoag women planted large gardens of corn, beans, squash, and pumpkins near their villages. Corn supplied most of their food, although

the men supplemented it with deer and bear meat and fish and shellfish.

The men wore buckskin breechcloths; the women wore short leather skirts. In cold weather they added fur robes and moccasins.

The Wampanoag believe that their god, Manitou, controls the forces of the universe and that when they die their souls will travel west to be with him.

Many Wampanoag died in a devastating epidemic that killed most of the coastal Indians in the early 1600s. They welcomed the early white settlers who came to Plymouth and helped them through their first winter. They were eager to have them as allies against their enemies, the Narragansett. For fifty years the settlers and the Wampanoag remained friends. Then the settlers began to move westward, cutting down trees, driving away game, and trampling precious wild plants. It was not long before many other tribes besides the Wampanoag began to feel the pain of hunger, which made them hostile to the settlers. Metacomet, son of Massasoit, the Native American who had greeted, nurtured, and maintained peace for Plymouth Colony, became chief of the tribe soon after his father died. Metamomet, better known as King

Philip, was angered by the death of his older brother, Alexander, who died mysteriously while visiting the colonists. In response to his brother's sudden death and the general unrest among the Indians, Metacomet convinced his people to ally themselves with their old enemies, the Narragansett. Between 1675 and 1676 many New England tribes burned and destroyed colonial settlements. The period is often called King Philip's War. The colonists allied themselves with the Mohegan, Pequot, Niantic, Sakonnet, and Massachusetts tribes, who helped to ambush and kill Metacomet, thus ending the uprising. After the war, Native Americans were rounded up, even if they had not taken part in the war, and sent to an island off Boston Harbor where many died. Some of them escaped, but others, including Metacomet's wife and son, were sold as slaves in the West Indies.

Descendants of the Wampanoag live on the island of Martha's Vineyard and in Cape Cod communities. They are presently seeking settlement of four hundred twenty-five acres of land in Gay Head on Martha's Vineyard, a small part of their original homeland.

WESTERN SHOSHONE

(sho-SHO-nee)

MEANING OF NAME: Unknown

CULTURE AREA: Great Basin

LOCATION: Northern Nevada and Utah

DWELLING TYPE: Conical shelters

CLOTHING MATERIALS: Bark and skins

TRANSPORTATION: Unknown

FOOD: Wild plants and meat

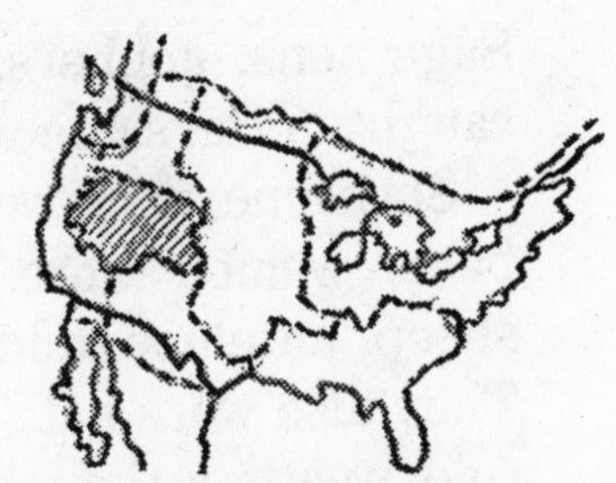

The Western Shoshone lived on the dry desert lands of Death Valley and in the mountains of central Nevada and northwestern Utah. Food resources throughout the region were limited, so they traveled all year gathering piñon seeds, mesquite pods, and wild wheat, and hunting bighorn sheep, antelope, and deer. They built conical huts, which they framed with poles and covered with slabs of bark. The Western Shoshone and their neighbors, the Gosiute Shoshone, shared a similar lifestyle. They traveled in small groups and owned a few horses.

The women used oval beaters to knock tiny seeds into finely woven gathering baskets. The men often organized communal rabbit hunts during which they hurled throwing-sticks at their prey to kill it. The rabbits were also driven into nets, snares, and traps.

BARK HUT

WOMAN WITH PACK BASKET AND SEED BEATER

CEREMONIAL PIPE

Sage hens, gophers, and squirrels were occasionally caught in the same way.

Shoshone men wore breechcloths of fur or woven bark; women wore skirts made of skins, favoring sheep, antelope, and deer when these were available. They also wore hats woven of sage bark or willow. In cold weather they both wore rabbit-skin robes and capes. Sometimes they decorated their faces and bodies with paint and tattoos.

The Western Shoshone believe they have a direct relationship with supernatural beings and can obtain power through visions and dreams. They hold dances to celebrate the piñon harvest and the rabbit season.

Between 1847 and 1863 white settlers trespassed onto the Western Shoshone land and disturbed their fragile food cycle, causing them great hunger. Mormon settlers took away most of the Indians' land and converted some of the Gosiute to Mormonism. Indians who would not be converted went to live with other Shoshone bands, and others stayed near Salt Lake City.

The Western Shoshone have filed a suit against the United States Government and are now seeking legal means to get back some of their homeland.

WINNEBAGO

(win-eh-BAY-go)

MEANING OF NAME: Muddy water people

CULTURE AREA: Northeast

LOCATION: Wisconsin

DWELLING TYPE: Bark- or mat-covered wigwams

CLOTHING MATERIAL: Skins

TRANSPORTATION: Snowshoes and bark canoes

FOOD: Meat, wild rice, fish, and wild plants

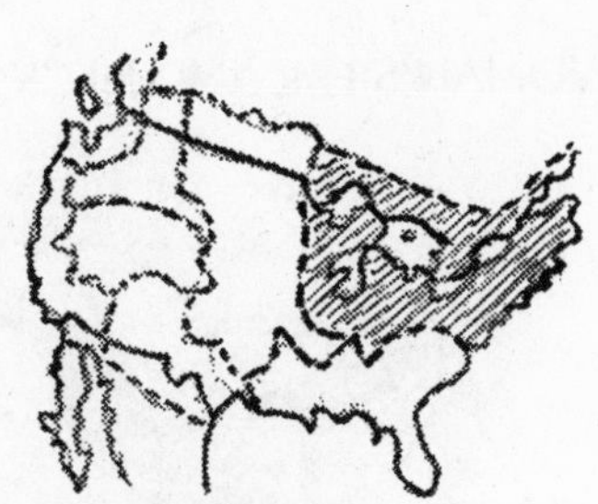

The Winnebago lived along the shores of Green Bay, fed by the swiftly flowing waters of the Menominee, Oconto, Wolf, and Fox rivers. Deer, bear, and buffalo once roamed the surrounding hills and sandy plains, and fish filled the rivers and streams. Wild rice flourished abundantly in shallow waters. The Winnebago built round, dome-shaped wigwams, which they framed with saplings and covered with bark or mats. They arranged them in a circle around a Council House.

Meat and wild rice supplied the Winnebago with most of their food. Their women planted small gardens of corn, beans, and squash, but they could not depend upon these crops because there is such a short growing season in this northern region.

The men wore deerskin breechcloths; the women wore short wraparound skirts. In cold weather they

WOMAN'S EAR AND NECK ORNAMENTS

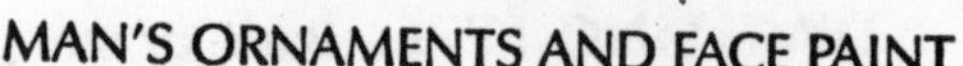

MAN'S ORNAMENTS AND FACE PAINT

WOODEN CEREMONIAL BOWL

WIGWAM

both added buckskin leggings, moccasins, and hooded fur capes.

The Winnebago traveled on snowshoes in winter. The rest of the year they used lightweight birch-bark canoes, which the men made by building a wooden frame and forming bark around it.

The Winnebago worship many gods, including Earthmaker, who created Sun, Moon, and Water, each a spirit god.

The Winnebago resisted proposals from early French trappers to trap furs for them, but they still caught white men's diseases, which killed many of them. They lost many more of their warriors fighting neighboring tribes. When bands of Algonquian-speaking Indians moved into the area to escape the Iroquois, the Winnebago survivors welcomed them and quickly adopted their customs. Later, when lead ore was discovered on Winnebago land, the Indians were forced to move to Minnesota, where they built farms and adopted European customs. In 1859, however, this land too was taken away, and they were moved in the middle of a cold winter to South Dakota. The trek took the lives of over five hundred Indians. Those who refused to leave Wisconsin were rounded up periodically and forcibly sent to South Dakota. Eventually government officials allowed the Winnebago to buy homestead sites in Wisconsin, but these were later lost because of unpaid taxes. Government policy at that time gave the Winnebago twenty-five years to eradicate their cultural and religious traditions and become Americanized. After that, they were expected to pay taxes like everyone else, or lose their land.

Descendants of the Winnebago live in Nebraska and Wisconsin.

WINTU

(WIN-tuh)

MEANING OF NAME: Person

CULTURE AREA: California

LOCATION: Northern California

DWELLING TYPE: Conical brush-covered shelters

CLOTHING MATERIALS: Skins and bark

TRANSPORTATION: Unknown

FOOD: Fish, meat, acorns, and wild plants

The Wintu lived in the valleys of the upper Trinity River from Mount Shasta in northern California to Cottonwood Creek in the south. They fished in the rivers, hunted in nearby mountains, and gathered wild plants all year. They built large permanent villages, usually of about one hundred and fifty people. They lived in conical houses which they framed with saplings and covered with evergreen boughs and bark. They arranged them around a large sweat house. The foundation of the sweat house was dug below ground and the upper portion was framed and covered like their houses. It was used only by the men for bathing and socializing.

The Wintu followed an annual cycle of food gathering. The men netted and speared several species of spawning salmon, they smoked brown bears from their dens when the animals were fat and sluggish, they herded deer and elk into enclosures using specially trained dogs, and they held communal rabbit hunts. Wintu families camped in the dense oak tree groves each fall, collecting acorn nuts, which were an important food source.

The men wore no clothing or they wore only skin breechcloths; the women wore shredded maple-bark aprons and basketlike hats. They both wore soft deerskin aprons and shirts for special occasions and deerskin and rabbit-skin capes when it was cold.

The Wintu worship Great Man or Above Person, and they believe that people are part wild animal and

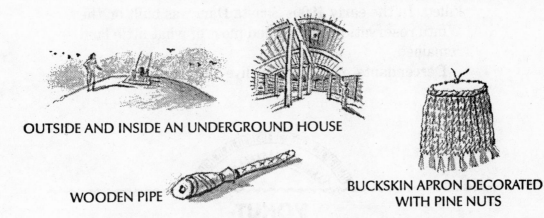

OUTSIDE AND INSIDE AN UNDERGROUND HOUSE

WOODEN PIPE

BUCKSKIN APRON DECORATED WITH PINE NUTS

part human, with souls that journey along a spirit trail, the Milky Way, when they die. They also believe that guardian spirits live behind people's ears and help them to think, feel, sleep, and get up in the morning.

In 1846 the Mexican Government granted portions of Wintu land to a rancher, whose cattle and sheep destroyed much of the area's wild food. Later, gold was discovered in the region and miners polluted the streams and forced the Indians to work the mines. In the mid-1850s a group of white settlers in Shasta County hosted a feast for the Wintu and put poison in the food. One hundred Wintu died at the feast. The survivors tried to warn another group not to share a feast with neighboring whites, but it was too late. Forty-five more natives died from poisoned food. Later the settlers dynamited a natural rock bridge traversing Clear Creek to keep the Wintu from crossing. They burned a Council House and killed three hundred more Indians. The survivors signed a treaty giving up all but a small piece of their land, but miners ignored the treaty and moved onto that land too. Before government troops arrived to enforce the treaty and protect the Indians, several hundred Wintu had been killed. In the early 1900s Shasta Dam was built on the Wintu reservation and flooded most of what little land remained.

Descendants of the Wintu live throughout California.

YOKUT
(YO-kut)

MEANING OF NAME: People
CULTURE AREA: California
LOCATION: Central California
DWELLING TYPE: Mat-covered round houses
CLOTHING MATERIAL: Skins
TRANSPORTATION: Leaf rafts
FOOD: Acorns, fish, meat, and wild plants

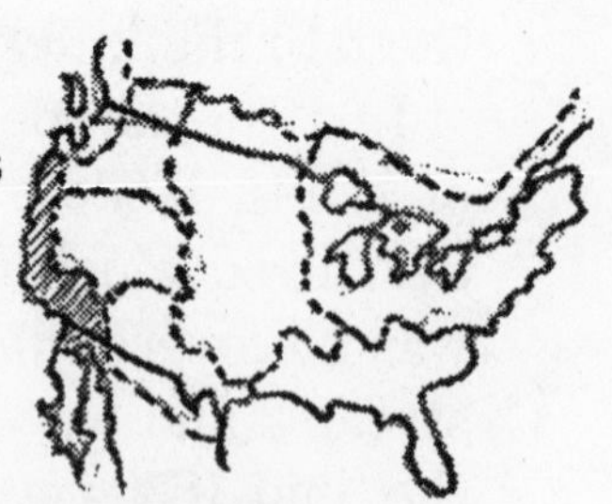

The Yokut lived in California in the San Joaquin Valley and along the western slopes of the Sierra Nevada Mountains. They hunted, fished, and gathered wild foods from the lower Kings River to the Tehachapi Mountains in the north, and along Tulare, Buena Vista, and Kern lakes in the south. Many rivers passed over the treeless land and emptied into shallow basins, creating vast marshlands. A species of bullrush, called tule, filled the marshland and supplied the Yokut with material for covering their houses, making clothes, and weaving baskets. The rich food resources of the

area allowed them to build large, permanent villages near the water. They built rows of round, steep-roofed houses which they framed with posts and covered with tule mats. Up to ten families lived in each house. Some groups built oval single-family houses.

Acorns provided the Yokut with most of their food. Men fished for trout, salmon, and a variety of other fish and hunted antelope, deer, elk, ducks, geese, hens, and jackrabbits in the Sierra foothills.

The men wore no clothing or only deerskin breechcloths; the women wore two-sided, woven-fiber aprons, made longer in the back than in the front, and basket-like caps. They both wore fur robes in cold weather and deer- and elk-skin moccasins when traveling in the mountains.

The Yokut built rafts by tying bulrush leaves into bundles, then tying the bundles together to form flat rafts. They used these rafts for transportation through the marshlands and streams.

The Yokut believe animals turn into people, and that Coyote caused an eclipse when he ate the moon. They employ shamans to help cure sickness and perform important ceremonies.

The Spaniards forced the Yokut to work in coastal missions beginning in 1722 and many died from disease, overwork, and lack of adequate food. Some escaped from the missions and joined other runaways, who raided local ranches. The Mexican government converted the missions to parish churches and took away the authority of the missionaries. A severe epidemic swept through central California in 1833 killing seventy-five percent of the native population. Survivors signed a treaty ceding their land in exchange for a reservation, but the treaty was never ratified, so the Yokut were forced to work for white ranchers and farmers. Eventually the government gave them small tracts of land in California.

Descendants of the Yokut live on the Tule River and Santa Rosa reservations or in southern California communities.

ZUNI

(ZOO-nee)

MEANING OF NAME: Unknown

CULTURE AREA: Southwest

LOCATION: Western New Mexico

DWELLING TYPE: Multifamily adobe houses

CLOTHING MATERIALS: Skins and cotton

TRANSPORTATION: Unknown

FOOD: Corn, meat, and wild plants

The Zuni who called themselves "the flesh," lived along the banks of the Zuni River west of the Continental Divide. The Zuni is a tributary of the Little Colorado River. Nearby, the Zuni Mountains rise nine thousand feet in the air, catching westerly flowing moisture and turning it into snow. Annual rains and melting snows gave the Indians a well-watered valley in which to raise crops. They built their first villages in the river valley, but during the Pueblo Revolt of 1680, they moved to mesa tops for protection against Spanish invasions. Only one village remains today on a mesa, but it has been occupied for more than three hundred and fifty years. It has five-story, multifamily adobe houses connected like apartments. Each family's living quarters are separated by a terrace, which becomes the roof of the house beneath it. Ladders enable the inhabitants to climb from one level to another.

Zuni men grew large crops of corn, beans, squash, and cotton. Corn supplied most of their food. The Spanish taught them to grow wheat and peaches and to raise sheep and burros. The Zuni continued to hunt deer and antelope and to conduct communal rabbit hunts, when they would stun the animals by hurling throwing-sticks.

The Zuni men wore woven cotton shirts, breeches, and skin leggings; the women wore one-piece cotton dresses tied over one shoulder and belted at the waist. They both wore skin moccasins.

POTTER

FORMAL CLOTHING, c. 1800

ADOBE HOUSES

Zuni boys are initiated into the Katchina Society before they are fourteen years old. They learn to impersonate rain spirits by wearing carved wooden masks. During the Winter Solstice priests wearing twelve-foot masks come to bless the occupants of the villages.

Spanish missionaries, who came to save the souls of the people and profit by the sweat of their bodies, built a mission in 1643 at Halona, the site of the Zuni main village. They worked the Zuni very hard and made large profits from native crops and from selling their handiwork in Europe and Mexico. The Spanish severely punished the Zuni for practicing their native religion, which encouraged many Indians to join the Pueblo Revolt in 1680 to drive away the Spanish. The Zuni and the Hopi, who received land grants from the Spanish Crown, were the only pueblo groups whose land was not invaded by American settlers in the 1800s. As a result, their original land grant became their reservation boundaries.

The Zuni still live in their ancient pueblo and in nearby communities.

Appendix

Major Tribes of North America

SOUTHEAST

Alabama
Apalachee
Caddo
Calusa
Catawba
Cherokee
Chickahominy
Chickasaw
Chitamacha
Choctaw
Creek
Hitchiti
Mikasuki
Mobile
Natchez
Oconee
Seminole
Yamasee

SOUTHWEST

Acoma
Cochiti
Havasupi
Hopi
Isleta
Jemez
Laguna
Maricopa
Navajo
Papago
Picuris
Pima
San Felipe
San Ildefonso
San Juan
Santa Ana
Santa Clara
Santo Domingo
Tewa
Tesque
Zia
Zuni

PLAINS

Apache
Apsaroke
Arapaho
Arikara
Assiniboin
Blackfoot
Blood
Brule
Cheyenne
Comanche
Crow
Gos Ventre
Hidatsa

Hunkpapa
Kansa
Kiowa
Loup
Mandan
Missouri
Oglala
Omaha
Osage
Oto
Pawnee
Piegan
Ponca
Sans Arc
Santee
Sarsi
Siksika
Sisseton
Skidi
Teton
Tonkawa
Waco
Wichita
Wolf
Yankton

GREAT BASIN

Boise Shoshone
Bruneau Shoshone
Chemehuevi
Eastern Shoshone
Fort Hall Shoshone
Gosiute Shoshone
Kawaiisu
Lemhi Shoshone
Northern Paiute
Northern Shoshone and
Bannock
Owens Valley Paiute
Panamint
Southern Paiute
Ute
Washoe
Western Shoshone

PLATEAU

Cour d'Alene
Flathead
Kutenai
Nez Perce
Suswap
Umatilla
Wallawalla
Yakima

NORTHWEST

Bella Coola
Chinook
Chehalis
Cowlitz
Dwamish
Haida
Klallam
Kwakiutl
Makah
Nootka
Quinault
Tlingit
Tsimshian

CALIFORNIA

Cahuilla
Chumush

Esselen
Gabrielino
Hupa
Karok
Klamath
Luiseno
Maidu
Miwok
Modoc
Mohave
Patwin
Pomo
Salina
Serrano
Shasta
Yokuts
Yurok
Yuma
Wintu

NORTHEAST

Abenaki
Algonquian
Amoskeag
Cayuga
Chippewa (Ojibwa)
Cree
Delaware
Erie
Fox
Kennebec
Kickapoo
Maliseet
Massachusetts
Menominee
Micmac
Mohawk
Mohegan
Montagnias
Nanticook
Narragansett
Nasaway
Niantic
Oneida
Onondaga
Ottawa
Passamaquoddy
Pennacook
Pennobscot
Pequot
Potawatomi
Sauk
Saulteaux
Seneca
Shawnee
Susquehana
Tuscarora
Wampanoag
Winnebago

Glossary

Acorns: The nuts, or fruits, gathered from oak trees. Six different varieties of oak tree grew in the state of California and acorns were very plentiful. Acorns are easy to gather and store because the hard casing around the nutmeat is a natural container. The Indians removed the "meat" from inside of the acorn and pounded it into flour. Acorn flour contained a poisonous substance called tannin, which the Indians leached out by pouring gallons of fresh water over the ground-up flour before it was cooked.

Adobe: A claylike soil used to make sun-dried bricks or applied like plaster to houses in the desert Southwest. Adobe soils contain just the right amount of sand, gravel, and clay, which when mixed can be molded and formed into durable bricks that will not warp or crack.

Allotment Act: Passed by Congress in 1887, the Allotment Act (Dawes Act) was designed to reduce the size of reservation land given to Indians sent west of the Mississippi River. It gave tribe members parcels of their reservation land and the government the right to sell the remaining land to white settlers.

Bark canoe: This lightweight boat was made by driving a row of posts into the ground to create a form, placing rolls of bark inside the form, and weighing the bark down with rocks. The boat was fitted with ribs, rails, and gunwales pegged into place and sewed with split spruce roots. Indian tribes preferred to make their canoes out of birch bark, but when it was not available, they used hickory, elm, and linden bark.

Bullboat: A small, round boat made by stretching animal hides, usually of buffalo, over a wooden frame. It was used to ferry women, children, and family belongings across swollen rivers and streams.

Candlefish: A small freshwater fish, also called olachen, caught in the Pacific Northwest in churning river waters that rush into the sea. These little fish are rich in oil, and it is said when a dried fish is lit it will burn like a candle.

Ceding of land: The Indians were made to sign papers that transferred the title or ownership of their land to the United States Government or its agents. Most Indians did not understand what owning land meant, however, and even if they had, the land could not have been surrendered without approval of the entire tribe—something that never happened.

Dugout Canoe: A sturdy wooden boat made by burning and scraping the center from large logs or tree trunks. The log was made nearly hollow, leaving the bottom and sides less than two inches thick. The bow and stern were often elaborately carved and sometimes painted. Many Indians made dugout canoes of pine, cedar, and cypress.

Earth Lodge: A large dwelling framed with huge timbers and covered with grass, soil, or sod. The foundations of these lodges were often dug out below ground.

False Face Society: A religious organization whose members wear grotesquely carved wooden masks that depict spirits seen in the forest or in people's dreams. Members become so powerful when wearing the masks that they can handle hot coals without getting burned. The masks have powers of their own and must have tobacco burned as a token of respect for them from time to time.

Five Civilized Tribes: The Cherokee, Creek, Chickasaw, Choctaw, and Seminole were the first tribes to be removed from their homelands in the East after passage of the Indian Removal Act in 1830. They were all sent to live on reservations west of the Mississippi River in Indian Territory. They suffered many losses in their trek westward. When Oklahoma sought statehood in 1907, the government of the Five Civilized tribes was dissolved, and their reservation land was reduced in size.

Ghost Dance: In 1888 a Paiute medicine man named Wovoka had a vision during which he learned how to teach other Indians to dance the Ghost Dance. Ghost Dance celebrations promised the Indians an end to white settlement and destruction of the environment. It gave them hope that their dead would return and restore the land and its resources through supernatural means. Promising a return to Indian ways, the Ghost Dance movement spread west to the Pacific coast, and east across the Great Plains. Ghost Dancing ended in 1890 at Wounded Knee, South Dakota, because the United States Army did not understand why the tribes had assembled, and killed most of the dancers.

Hogan: A Navajo dwelling framed with large piñon pine logs and covered with brush, earth, and soil. Construction of a hogan, which always faced east, required a number of rituals.

Homestead Act: Passed in 1862, it opened for settlement land given to the Indians west of the Mississippi in Kansas and Nebraska. White settlers, called homesteaders, received 160-acre plots of land with the proviso that they live on the land for at least five years.

Indian Removal Act: Passed by Congress in 1830, it called for relocation of all Indians living in the East to be removed to reservations west of the Mississippi River, which was Indian Territory.

Indian Territory: Considered wilderness in 1820, it was all of the land west of the Mississippi River. By 1850 Indian Territory was at its largest and it extended from the Red River to the

Missouri River and from the present-day state lines of Arkansas, Mississippi, and Iowa to the 100th meridian. The northern part of this territory later became the states of Kansas and Nebraska.

Katchinas: Masked dancers who visit villages once a year wearing brightly carved and painted wooden masks depicting rain gods. The masked katchinas dance to bring rain. Children are given small carved versions of the rain gods to take home to study.

League of Six Nations or Iroquois Confederacy: Members included the Cayuga, Seneca, Onondaga, Oneida, Mohawk, and Tuscarora. The League was founded by a Huron mystic named Deganawida, and his disciple, Hiawatha, between A.D. 1400 and 1600 and was organized to stop intertribal warfare. A council of great chiefs, chosen from members of the five original tribes, drew up laws and decided upon customs, which would be maintained by League members.

Longhouse: A long, rectangular dwelling framed with posts and covered with large sheets of bark, or a barrel-shaped longhouse built by pushing two long rows of thick saplings into the ground, bending them at the top and tying them together. Barrel-shaped longhouses were usually covered with bark or mats.

Oklahoma: Land west of the Mississippi River was designated by Congress as "Indian Territory," and was set aside for eastern Indians who were removed from their homeland. During the 1800s white settlers moved onto this land and soon demanded statehood. In 1907 most of the Indian Territory became the state of Oklahoma, and the land was divided among Indian tribes and white settlers.

Pemmican: A nutritious mixture of pounded, dried meat mixed with berries and nuts. It was packed into hide containers and fat was poured over the top to make it last many months.

Plankhouse: Large rectangular dwellings framed with timbers and covered with vertical or horizontal cedar or spruce planks, built mostly along the Northwest Coast and northern California.

Potlatch: A party hosted each winter by an important or wealthy Northwest Coast Indian. Potlatches lasted several days and often celebrated an important event—a birth, a name-giving, an initiation ceremony, a marriage, or a death. Each host tried to outdo the others by giving away bigger and better gifts to his guests. Gifts of copper, shell, and woven blankets were important indicators of wealth and status. The richest and most important clans and groups, of course, gave the largest number of potlatches.

Pueblo Revolt of 1680: A Tewa medicine man named Pope staged a rebellion against harsh Spanish rule and religion in the Southwest. He was joined by other Pueblo tribes, who drove away the Spanish invaders.

Reservation: A parcel of land set aside for Indian people to live on.

Shaman: A religious person who seeks ways to control spirits through the use of magic, herbal cures, and a variety of rituals.

Smallpox: A devastating disease brought to the New World by European settlers, who had already developed immunity to this and to a number of other diseases. Thousands of Indians died from European diseases, which were spread throughout the land by white settlers.

Snowshoes: Designed to attach to heavy moccasins, these large round frames are made of readily available hardwood and woven with rawhide. In the wintertime, they were used to track animals through deep snow.

Spirit Deities: The Indians believed in many spirits, or gods, never in just one deity. They believed there were specific spirits that dwelled in or disguised themselves as water, trees, animals, or other living things. Manitou, Great Spirit, Gluscap, Raven, Trickster, Racoon, Wakan Tanka, and Earth Maker are the names of some of these spirits. The Indians also believed that a special supernatural force, or power, traveled throughout the universe and could be interrupted and used by people who had the proper knowledge and equipment to use it.

Texas Rangers: A group organized by Texas settlers to rid the region of Indians after Texas declared itself independent of Mexico in 1835.

Totems: Animal or natural objects believed to symbolize a family or clan.

Travois: An unwheeled, sledlike cart first attached to dogs to pull belongings and later attached to horses.

Treaty: A formal agreement between two or more nations, relating to peace or to an alliance. From 1835 to 1856 the United States signed 52 treaties with native Americans to acquire 174 million acres of land—and broke every one of them.

Wigwam: A round or elliptical dwelling made by pushing young, flexible saplings into the ground, bending them at the top, and tying them together. They were then covered with bark or mats.

Selected Bibliography

Abrams, George H. J. *The Seneca People.* Phoenix: Indian Tribal Series, 1976.

Bock, Wm. Sauts Netamuxwe. *The First Americans.* Wilmington, Delaware: The Middle Atlantic Press, 1974.

Brown, Douglas Summers. *The Catawba Indians: The People of the River.* Columbia, South Carolina: University of South Carolina Press, 1966.

Burt, Jesse, and Robert B. Fergeson. *Indians of the Southeast: Then and Now.* New York: Abingdon Press, 1973.

Carter, Samuel. *Cherokee Sunset.* Garden City, New Jersey: Doubleday and Co., 1976.

Chelfant, Stuart A. *Nez Perce Indians.* New York: Garland Publishing, Inc., 1974.

Danziger, Edmund Jefferson, Jr. *The Chippewas of Lake Superior.* Norman, Oklahoma: University of Oklahoma Press, 1978.

D'Azevedo, Warren L., ed. *Handbook of the North American Indians*, Vol. 11, *Great Basin.* Washington, D.C.: Smithsonian Institution, 1986.

Debo, Angie. *The Rise and Fall of the Choctaw Republic.* Norman, Oklahoma: University of Oklahoma Press, 1934.

DeRosier, Arthur H. Jr. *The Removal of the Choctaw Indians.* Knoxville, Tennessee: University of Tennessee Press, 1970.

Douglas, F. H. *Indian Women's Clothing: Fashion and Function.* Leaflet 109. Colorado: Denver Art Museum, 1956.

Fletcher, Alice C. and Frances LaFlesche. *The Omaha Tribe.* Vol. II. Lincoln, Nebraska: University of Nebraska Press, 1972.

Garbarino, Merwyn S. *Big Cypress: A Changing Seminole Community*. New York: Holt, Rinehart and Winston, Inc., 1972.

Gay, E. Jane. *With the Nez Perces, Alice Fletcher in the Field, 1889–92*. Lincoln, Nebraska: University of Nebraska Press, 1981.

Geographic Board of Canada. *Handbook of Indians of Canada*. Toronto, Canada: Coles Publishing Company, 1971.

Gibson, A. M. *The Kickapoos: Lords of the Middle Border*. Norman, Oklahoma: The University of Oklahoma Press, 1963.

——— *The Chickasaws*. 1971.

Gilpin, Laura. *The Enduring Navaho*. Austin, Texas: University of Texas Press, 1968.

Grinnell, George Bird. *When Buffalo Ran*. New Haven: Yale University Press, 1920.

Heizer, Robert F., ed. *Handbook of North American Indians*, Vol. 8, *California*. Washington, D.C.: Smithsonian Institution, 1978.

Helm, June, ed. *Handbook of North American Indians*, Vol. 6, *Subarctic*. Washington, D.C.: Smithsonian Institution, 1981.

Hudson, Charles. *The Southeastern Indians*. Knoxville, Tennessee: The University of Tennessee Press, 1976.

Jenness, Diamond. *The Indians of Canada*. Ottawa: National Museum of Canada, 1932.

Johnson, F. Roy. *The Tuscaroras*, 2 vols. Murfreesboro, North Carolina: Johnson Publishing Company, 1967–68.

Jones, Jayne Clark. *The American Indian in America*, Vol. 1. Minneapolis, Minnesota: Lerner Publications Co., 1973.

Kroeber, A. L. *Cultural and Natural Areas of Native North America*. Berkeley: University of California Press, 1953.

——— *Handbook of the Indians of California*. New York: Dover Publications, Inc. 1976.

Kroeber, Alfred L. *The Arapaho*. Lincoln, Nebraska: University of Nebraska Press, 1983.

Kroeber, Theodora and Robert F. Heizer. *Almost Ancestors. The First Californians*. New York: Sierra Club, 1968.

LaFarge, Oliver. *As Long as the Grass Shall Grow.* New York: Alliance Book Corporation, 1940.

Leitch, Barbara A. *A Concise Dictionary of Indian Tribes of North America.* Algonac, Michigan: Reference Publications, Inc., 1979.

Lowie, Robert H. *Indians of the Plains.* New York: The Natural History Press, 1954.

Madsen, Brigham D. *The Northern Shoshoni.* Caldwell, Idaho: The Caxton Printers, Ltd., 1980.

——— *The Bannock of Idaho.* Caldwell, Idaho: The Caxton Printers, Ltd., 1958.

McHugh, Tom. *The Time of the Buffalo.* Lincoln: University of Nebraska Press, 1972.

McReynolds, Edwin C. *The Seminoles.* Norman, Oklahoma: University of Oklahoma Press, 1957.

Morgan, Lewis H. *Houses and House-Life of the American Aborigines.* Chicago: University of Chicago Press, 1965.

Neill, Wilfred T. *Florida's Seminole Indians.* St. Petersbury, Florida, 1976.

Newcomb, W. W. Jr. *The Indians of Texas.* Austin, Texas: University of Texas Press, 1961.

Ortiz, Alfonso, ed. *Handbook of North American Indians,* Vol. 9, *Southwest.* Washington, D.C.: Smithsonian Institution, 1979.

——— *Handbook of North American Indians,* Vol. 10, *Southwest.* Washington, D.C.: Smithsonian Institution, 1983.

Radin, Paul. *The Winnebago Tribe,* 1923. Reprint. New York: Johnson Reprint Corp., 1970.

Richards, Cara E. *The Oneida People.* Phoenix: Indian Tribal Series, 1974.

Rickman, David. *Northwest Coast Indians.* New York: Dover Publications, 1984.

——— *Plains Indians.* New York: Dover Publications, 1983.

Ritzenthaler, Robert E. and Pat Ritzenthaler. *The Woodland Indi-*

ans of the Western Great Lakes. Milwaukee: American Museum Science Books, 1970.

Rockwell, Wilson. *The Utes: A Forgotten People.* Denver: Sage Books, 1956.

Rosier, Arthur H. Jr. *The Removal of the Choctaw Indians.* Knoxville, Tennessee: University of Tennessee Press, 1970.

Ruby, Robert H. and John A. Brown. *A Guide to the Indian Tribes of the Pacific Northwest.* Norman, Oklahoma: University of Oklahoma Press, 1986.

Sharpe, J. Ed. *The Cherokee Past and Present: An Authentic Guide to the Cherokee People.* Cherokee, North Carolina: Cherokee Publications, 1970.

Terrell, John Upton. *Sioux Trail.* New York: McGraw Hill, 1974.

Trigger, Bruce G. *Handbook of North American Indians,* Vol. 15, *Northeast.* Washington, D.C.: Smithsonian Institution, 1978.

Underhill, Ruth M. *Red Man's America.* Chicago: The University of Chicago Press, 1953.

——— *First Penthouse Dwellers of America.* Santa Fe, New Mexico: Laboratory of Anthropology, 1946.

U.S. Department of the Interior, Bureau of Indian Affairs. *Indians of the Great Lakes.* Washington, D.C.: U.S. Government Printing Office, 1968.

U.S. Department of the Interior, Bureau of Indian Affairs. *Indians of Oklahoma.* Washington, D.C.: U.S. Government Printing Office, 1986.

Vernon, Howard A. *The Cayuga Claims.* A Background Study. American Indian Culture and Research Journal, Vol. 4, No. 3. Los Angeles: American Indian Studies Center, 1980.

Waldman, Carl. *Atlas of the North American Indian.* New York: Facts on File Publication, 1985.

Wallace, Anthony F. S. *The Death and Rebirth of the Seneca.* New York: Alfred A. Knopf, 1969.

Wallace, Ernest and E. Adamson Hoebel. *The Comanches: Lords of the South Plains*. Norman, Oklahoma: University of Oklahoma Press, 1952.

Weslager, C. A. *The Delaware Indians*. New Brunswick, New Jersey: Rutgers University Press, 1972.

Wilson, Edmund. *Apologies to the Iroquois*. New York: Farrar, Straus, Cudahy, 1960.

Wissler, Clark. *Indians of the United States: Four Centuries of Their History and Culture*. New York: Doubleday, Doran & Company, Inc., 1940.

Suggested Reading

Ashabranner, Brent. *To Live in Two Worlds: American Indian Youth Today*. New York: Dodd Mead, 1984.

Bock, Wm. Sauts Netamuxwe. *The First Americans*. Wilmington, Delaware: The Middle Atlantic Press, 1974.

D'Azevedo, Warren L. ed. *Handbook of the North American Indians*, Vol. 11. *Great Basin*. Washington, D.C.: Smithsonian Institution, 1986.

Douglas, F. H. *Indian Women's Clothing: Fashion and Function*. Leaflet 109. Colorado: Denver Art Museum, 1956.

Freedman, Russell. *Indian Chiefs*. New York: Holiday House, Inc., 1987.

Garbarino, Merwyn S. *Big Cypress: A Changing Seminole Community*. New York: Holt, Rinehart and Winston, Inc., 1972.

Gates, Frieda. *North American Indian Masks*. New York: Walker and Company, 1982.

Gilpin, Laura. *The Enduring Navaho*. Austin, Texas: University of Texas Press, 1968.

Heizer, Robert F., ed. *Handbook of North American Indians*, Vol. 8, *California*. Washington, D.C.: Smithsonian Institution, 1978.

Helm, June, ed. *Handbook of North American Indians*, Vol. 6, *Subarctic*. Washington, D.C.: Smithsonian Institution, 1981.

Highwater, Jamake. *Arts of the Indian Americas*. New York: Harper & Row, Publishers, 1983.

Hirshfelder, Arlene. *Happily May I Walk: American Indians and Alaskan Natives Today*. New York: Charles Scribners Sons, 1986.

Kazimizoff, Theordore. *The Last Algonquin*. New York: Walker and Company, 1982.

Kessel, Joyce K. *Squanto and the First Thanksgiving*. Minneapolis, Minnesota: Carolrhoda Books, 1983.

LaFarge, Oliver. *As Long as the Grass Shall Grow*. New York: Alliance Book Corporation, 1940.

Logan, Adelphena. *Memories of Sweetgrass*. Washington, Connecticut: American Indian Archaeological Institute, Inc., 1979.

Lowie, Robert H. *Indians of the Plains*. New York: Natural History Press, 1954.

Madsen, Brigham D. *The Northern Shoshoni*. Caldwell, Idaho: The Caxton Printers, Ltd., 1980.

——— *The Bannock of Idaho*. Caldwell, Idaho: The Caxton Printers, Ltd., 1958.

McHugh, Tom. *The Time of the Buffalo*. Lincoln, Nebraska: University of Nebraska Press, 1972.

Neill, Wilfred T. *Florida's Seminole Indians*. St. Petersburg, Florida, 1976.

Newcomb, W. W., Jr. *The Indians of Texas*. Austin, Texas: University of Texas Press, 1961.

Ortiz, Alfonso, editor. *Handbook of North American Indians*, Vol. 9, *Southwest*. Washington, D.C.: Smithsonian Institution, 1979.

——— ed. *Handbook of North American Indians*, Vol. 10, *Southwest*. Washington, D.C.: Smithsonian Institution, 1983.

Rickman, David. *Northwest Coast Indians*. New York: Dover Publications, 1984.

——— *Plains Indians*. New York: Dover Publications, 1983.

Sharpe, J. Ed. *The Cherokee Past and Present: An Authentic Guide to the Cherokee People*. Cherokee, North Carolina: Cherokee Publications, 1970.

Simon, Nancy and Evelyn Wolfson. *American Indian Habitats*. New York: David McKay Co., Inc., 1978.

Trigger, Bruce B. *Handbook of North American Indians*, Vol. 15, *Northeast*. Washington, D.C.: Smithsonian Institution, 1978.

Waldman, Carl. *Atlas of the North American Indian.* New York: Facts on File Publication, 1985.

Wallin, Luke. *Ceremony of the Panther.* New York: Bradbury Press, 1987.

Wolfson, Evelyn. *American Indian Utensils.* New York: David McKay Co., Inc., 1979.

——— *American Indian Tools and Ornaments.* New York: David McKay Co., Inc. 1981.

——— *Growing Up Indian.* New York: Walker and Company, 1986.

Index

18218

973.004 Wolfson, Evelyn
Wol
From Abenaki to Zuni

DATE DUE

ORISKANY HIGH SCHOOL LIBRARY